REVISE AQA GCSE
German

D1381798

REVISION WORKBOOK

Series Consultant: Harry Smith

Author: Harriette Lanzer

Also available to support your revision:

Revise GCSE Study Skills Guide   9781447967071

The **Revise GCSE Study Skills Guide** is full of tried-and-trusted hints and tips for how to learn more effectively. It gives you techniques to help you achieve your best – throughout your GCSE studies and beyond!

Revise GCSE Revision Planner   9781447967828

The **Revise GCSE Revision Planner** helps you to plan and organise your time, step-by-step, throughout your GCSE revision. Use this book and wall chart to mastermind your revision.

For the full range of Pearson revision titles across GCSE, BTEC and AS Level visit:

www.pearsonschools.co.uk/revise

Contents

LIFESTYLE
1 Birthdays
2 Pets
3 Physical description
4 Character description
5 Brothers and sisters
6 Family
7 Friends
8 Daily routine
9 Breakfast
10 Eating at home
11 Eating in a café
12 Eating in a restaurant
13 Healthy eating
14 Health issues
15 Health problems
16 Future relationship plans
17 Social issues
18 Social problems

LEISURE
19 General hobbies
20 Sport
21 Arranging to go out
22 What I did last weekend
23 TV programmes
24 Cinema
25 Music
26 New technology
27 Language of the internet
28 Internet pros and cons
29 Shops
30 Food shopping
31 Shopping
32 Clothes and colours
33 Buying clothes
34 Returning clothes
35 Shopping opinions
36 Pocket money
37 Holiday destinations
38 Holiday accommodation
39 Booking accommodation
40 Staying in a hotel
41 Staying on a campsite
42 Holiday activities
43 Holiday preferences
44 Holiday plans
45 Past holidays

HOME AND ENVIRONMENT
46 Countries
47 My house
48 My room
49 Helping at home
50 Where I live
51 Places in town
52 What to do in town
53 Tourist attractions
54 Signs in town
55 Pros and cons of your town
56 Town description
57 Weather
58 Celebrations at home
59 Directions
60 At the train station
61 Travelling
62 Transport
63 The environment
64 Environmental issues
65 What I do to be 'green'
66 News headlines

WORK AND EDUCATION
67 School subjects
68 Opinions about school
69 School routine
70 German schools
71 Primary school
72 Rules at school
73 School problems
74 Future education plans
75 Future careers
76 Jobs
77 Job adverts
78 CV
79 Job application
80 Job interview
81 Opinions about jobs
82 Part-time work
83 Work experience
84 My work experience

GRAMMAR
85 Gender and plurals
86 Cases 1
87 Cases 2
88 Cases 3
89 Adjective endings
90 Comparisons
91 Personal pronouns
92 Word order
93 Conjunctions
94 More on word order
95 The present tense
96 More on verbs
97 Commands
98 Present tense modals
99 Imperfect modals
100 The perfect tense 1
101 The perfect tense 2
102 The imperfect tense
103 The future tense
104 The conditional
105 The pluperfect tense
106 Questions
107 Time markers
108 Numbers

109 Practice Exam Paper: Reading
114 Practice Exam Paper: Listening
120 Answers

Audio files

Audio files and transcripts for the listening exercises in this book can be found at: www.pearsonschools.co.uk/ mflrevisionaudio

A small bit of small print

AQA publishes Sample Assessment Material and the Specification on its website. This is the official content and this book should be used in conjunction with it. The questions in this book have been written to help you practise what you have learned in your revision. Remember: the real exam questions may not look like this.

Target grades

Target grades are quoted in this book for some of the questions. Students targeting this grade should be aiming to get some of the marks available. Students targeting a higher grade should be aiming to get all of the marks available.

Birthdays

When is your birthday?

1 Mia has made a note of friends' birthdays.

Julia	16. März
Marie	1. Juli
Kerim	14. Oktober
Sabine	24. Januar
Leni	11. Dezember
David	12. Mai
Peter	9. August
Olaf	30. April
Frank	20. Februar

> Start with the items you can do most easily.

Write the initial of the person: **J** (Julia), **M** (Marie), etc.

Example: Whose birthday is in January?   S

Whose birthday is in …

(a) May?   ☐   *(1 mark)*

(b) July?   ☐   *(1 mark)*

(c) March?   ☐   *(1 mark)*

(d) February?   ☐   *(1 mark)*

Birthday parties

Audio files
Audio files can be found at:
www.pearsonschools.co.uk/mflrevisionaudio

2 Listen to Mrs Schulz talking about how her family celebrates birthdays in different ways.

(a) What disadvantage of birthday parties does Mrs Schulz mention?
.... *(1 mark)*

(b) What did her husband buy her for her birthday yesterday?
.... *(1 mark)*

(c) When is Markus's birthday?
.... *(1 mark)*

(d) How did Sabine celebrate her birthday last year? Mention **two** things.

(i) .... *(1 mark)*

(ii) .... *(1 mark)*

(e) How did Mrs Schulz find the celebration?
.... *(1 mark)*

Pets

The animal home

3 You read this report about an animal rescue centre.

○ Seit sechs Jahren arbeitet Miriam in einer Tierarztpraxis in einer kleinen Stadt in Nordostdeutschland und sie findet es immer noch erstaunlich, dass jede Woche mindestens ein unerwünschtes Haustier vor der Tür gelassen wird.
„Das kann ein Kaninchen, ein Hund, eine Schlange oder ein Wellensittich sein "erklärt Miriam. „Oft fährt die Familie in den Urlaub und weiß nicht, was sie mit dem Haustier machen soll, also bringt man das Tier zu uns, weil das billig und schnell das Problem löst"

○ Der Manager der Praxis hat neulich einen Käfig und einen großen Karton neben die Haustür gestellt, wo Besitzer ihre Haustiere sicher lassen können. Ein Assistent der Praxis wäscht und füttert das Tier, bevor man es in ein größere Tierheim bringt, um es danach in eine neue Familie zu geben.

○ „Am Anfang des Neuen Jahres sind wir sehr beschäftigt," meint Miriam, „weil so viele Kinder sich zu Weihnachten ein Haustier wünschen, aber wenn das Tier ankommt, hat das Kind oft kein Interesse daran und hat überhaupt keine Lust zum Beispiel den Hund zu füttern oder auszuführen. Man braucht Zeit und Geduld, um auf ein Haustier richtig aufzupassen. Es ärgert mich am meisten, dass sich so viele Leute ein Haustier kaufen und es dann nicht richtig lieben."

Which **four** sentences are correct?

Write the **four** correct letters in the boxes.

Example:

[A] [ ] [ ] [ ] [ ]   *(4 marks)*

A	Miriam has been working at the animal home for six years.
B	Miriam is not surprised that people abandon their pets.
C	Owners come into the home to leave their pets.
D	Abandoned pets are sent straight away to a new family.
E	Some pets come to the animal home for their holiday.
F	The animal home often has to turn unwanted pets away.
G	Animals dropped off in the special box are fed and washed before going to a bigger animal home.
H	You need money and patience to look after a pet.
I	The busiest time for the animal home is New Year.

Ulrike's pet

4 Listen to Ulrike talking about her pet. Write the correct letter in the box.

(a) What pet does Ulrike have? [ ]

A [image]   B [image]   C [image]

(c) What is Ulrike's pet's personality? [ ]

A | aggressive   B | shy   C | lazy

(b) What colour is Ulrike's pet? [ ]

A [image]   B [image]   C [image]

(d) Where does Ulrike's pet sleep? [ ]

A [image]   B [image]   C [image]

(4 marks)

Physical description

Describing someone

5 Read the description of this wanted person.

> # WIR SUCHEN MICHAEL HENNING
>
> Er ist 1,70 m groß und sehr schlank. Er hat braune, glatte Haare und ein rundes Gesicht.
>
> Seine Augen sind grün und er trägt immer eine Brille. Er hat einen langen Bart.
>
> Er hat auch einen großen Ohrring im linken Ohr.

A	grey		D	long		G	short
B	curly		E	1.70 metres		H	straight
C	necklace		F	green		I	earring

What does Michael Henning look like? Write the correct letter from the above list in the box.

Example: His height E

(a) Hair style ☐ *(1 mark)*   (c) Style of beard ☐ *(1 mark)*

(b) Colour of eyes ☐ *(1 mark)*   (d) Jewellery ☐ *(1 mark)*

A new girlfriend

6 Listen to Christian talking about his new girlfriend. Write the correct letter in the box.

(a) Anna's hair is …

A	short and straight
B	long and curly
C	short and curly

☐ *(1 mark)*

(b) Her eyes are …

A	blue
B	brown
C	green

☐ *(1 mark)*

(c) She is …

A	15
B	16
C	17

☐ *(1 mark)*

(d) She wears …

A	glasses
B	glasses and earrings
C	earrings

☐ *(1 mark)*

(e) Her dog is …

A	friendly
B	small
C	big

☐ *(1 mark)*

3

Had a go ☐ Nearly there ☐ Nailed it! ☐

Character description

My brother Kadir

7   Emine describes her brother.

> Mein jüngerer Bruder Kadir ist ⟦K⟧ Jahre alt und wir verstehen uns wirklich gut. Als er sehr klein war, war er schüchtern und ziemlich ernst. Wenn ein Erwachsener ihm eine Frage stellte, musste ich als seine ☐ schwester die Frage immer beantworten. Ich fand ihn so lieb und ich wollte ihm immer helfen!
>
> Kadir ist jetzt sehr lustig und freundlich und er kommt allen gar nicht ☐ vor. Ich bin zwar ein bisschen faul, aber Kadir ist das nie, weil er immer so viel ☐ hat. In der Schule ist er besonders fleißig und er hat nie Probleme mit den Aufgaben. Obwohl er drei Jahre jünger ist als ich, hilft er mir sehr ☐ mit den Hausaufgaben, wenn ich Schwierigkeiten damit habe. Er findet immer Zeit für mich.
>
> Normalerweise ist Kadir gut gelaunt, aber ab und zu wird er recht böse, besonders wenn jemand ☐ ist – er kann es nicht leiden, wenn jemand zum Beispiel zum Busfahrer frech ist oder Abfall auf den Boden wirft.

Fill the gaps with a word from the table. Write the correct letter in the box.

A	geduldig
B	nett
C	Zwillings-
D	schüchtern
E	unhöflich
F	laut
G	Geld
H	ältere
I	Energie
J	intelligent
K	dreizehn

> The text before or after the gap will lead you to the answer, so make sure you read enough to find it.

(5 marks)

Penfriends' characteristics

8   Listen to Renate and Lukas talking about their penfriends. What do they think about them? Write the correct letter in the box.

A	Sporty	**B**	Bad tempered
C	Always in a good mood	**D**	Cheeky

(a) Lukas ☐   *(1 mark)*

(b) Renate ☐   *(1 mark)*

Brothers and sisters

Sophie's brothers and sisters

9 You read this profile in a magazine.

> Sophies Bruder ist sieben Jahre alt und ihre Schwester ist dreizehn. Sie muss ziemlich oft auf ihren Bruder aufpassen und sie findet ihn sehr lustig. Er ist manchmal ein bisschen frech, aber sie verstehen sich gut.
>
> Ihre Schwester geht ihr aber ganz auf die Nerven. Sie nimmt sich manchmal Sophies Sachen, zum Beispiel ihre Kleidung und CDs. Und sie spielt laute Musik, wenn Sophie lesen oder lernen will. Sie streiten sich die ganze Zeit.

A	kind		D	playing music		G	funny
B	annoying		E	a sister		H	well
C	badly		F	arguing		I	cheeky

Write the correct letter in the box to complete the sentences.

Example: Sophie has a brother and   **E**

(a) Her brother is sometimes   ☐ .   *(1 mark)*

(b) She and her brother generally get on   ☐ .   *(1 mark)*

(c) She finds her sister   ☐ .   *(1 mark)*

(d) She and her sister are always   ☐ .   *(1 mark)*

Alex's sister

10 Listen to Alex describing his relationship with his sister. Write the correct letter in the box.

(a) What relationship does Alex have with his sister?
- **A** Very good
- **B** They have shared hobbies
- **C** They argue a lot   ☐   *(1 mark)*

(b) What does Alex see as a problem?
- **A** His sister is younger than him
- **B** His sister is older than him
- **C** His sister plays with his toys   ☐   *(1 mark)*

(c) What does Alex think of his sister's TV programmes?
- **A** He enjoys them
- **B** He thinks they are OK
- **C** He thinks they are silly   ☐   *(1 mark)*

(d) Why does Alex think he should be allowed to watch his programmes?
- **A** Because he is the oldest
- **B** Because the TV is in his room
- **C** Because his sister prefers to play   ☐   *(1 mark)*

Family

Family life

11 You read this article in a newspaper.

> Obwohl ich Einzelkind bin, habe ich mich nie einsam gefühlt. Als ich in der Grundschule war, haben wir in Frankfurt gewohnt. In derselben Stadt waren meine Großeltern und meine Tanten, und es hat mir viel Spaß gemacht, regelmäßig mit meinen zwei Cousinen zu spielen.
>
> Weil meine Eltern bis spät am Abend arbeiten mussten, hat meine Tante Julia nach der Schule auf mich aufgepasst. Meine Tante ist ebenso streng wie Mutti und Vati, und ich musste immer Hausaufgaben machen, bevor ich spielen oder fernsehen durfte. Das war mir egal, weil mir meine Cousine oft geholfen hat, die Schularbeiten zu machen.
>
> Vor vier Jahren mussten wir nach Bonn ziehen, weil meine Eltern sich dort erfolgreich auf Stellen bei einer großen Firma beworben haben. Ich war sehr traurig, dass ich meine Umgebung sowie meine Cousinen verlassen musste und jetzt weit von ihnen entfernt wohne. Wir sehen uns zwar nicht so oft, aber wir können telefonieren oder SMS schicken. Außerdem organisiert meine Mutter während der Sommerferien oft einen Familienausflug. Jedes Jahr unternehmen wir etwas Neues und die ganze Familie macht mit, aber ich würde am allerliebsten doch nach Frankfurt zurückziehen.
>
> **Thomas (16)**

Read the following sentences. Write **T** (True), **F** (False) or **?** (Not in the text) in the box.

(a) Thomas is sometimes lonely because he doesn't have brothers and sisters. ☐ *(1 mark)*

(b) Thomas used to enjoy playing with his cousins. ☐ *(1 mark)*

(c) Thomas was born in Bonn. ☐ *(1 mark)*

(d) Thomas's aunt is not as strict as his parents. ☐ *(1 mark)*

(e) Thomas used to do his homework in front of the TV. ☐ *(1 mark)*

(f) Thomas was in the same class as his cousin. ☐ *(1 mark)*

(g) Thomas's parents went to Bonn to look for work. ☐ *(1 mark)*

(h) Thomas's cousins don't live near Bonn. ☐ *(1 mark)*

(i) Thomas would love to have family outings more than once a year. ☐ *(1 mark)*

> Make sure you learn prepositions to help you make sense of reading and listening passages.

Friends

My friends

12 These people are talking about their friends.

Ahmed ist treu und humorvoll. Er hilft gerne, wenn jemand ein Problem hat. **Max** ist ein guter Freund, aber er ist manchmal launisch. Er wird böse, wenn er ein Spiel nicht gewinnt. **Lena** ist sehr lustig, aber ziemlich blöd. Es ist gut, dass sie nie schlecht gelaunt ist und ich finde sie meistens nett. **Ralf** ist sehr intelligent, aber er kann in der Klasse schüchtern sein und er beantwortet nie die Fragen. Wir kommen gut miteinander aus.	**Hanna** ist sehr fleißig, aber das geht mir auf die Nerven, weil sie immer bessere Noten bekommt als ich! Sie arbeitet viel in der Schule und zu Hause. **Frank** liebt Musik, aber manchmal kann das langweilig sein, weil er am Computer sitzt und endlos Lieder herunterlädt. Er spielt Gitarre in einer Band und singt die ganze Zeit. **Petra** ist sehr sportlich. Ich kenne sie seit der Grundschule und ich finde sie sehr sympathisch, obwohl sie manchmal launisch ist.

Write the initial of the person: **A** (Ahmed), **M** (Max), etc.

> Be careful – there are always more texts to choose from than answers needed.

Example: Who is shy?   `R`

Who …

(a) is a bad loser? ☐ *(1 mark)*

(b) is happy to help others? ☐ *(1 mark)*

(c) works hard to get good grades? ☐ *(1 mark)*

(d) is never in a bad mood? ☐ *(1 mark)*

Melissa's school friends

13 Listen to Melissa talking about her old school friends.

(a) (i) Give an example of how Ivan was shy last year

.... *(1 mark)*

(ii) How has Melissa's attitude to him changed?

.... *(1 mark)*

(b) (i) What was Olivia's behaviour like in class last year? Give **two** examples.

....

.... *(2 marks)*

(ii) What reason is given for Olivia becoming friendlier?

.... *(1 mark)*

> There is often more than one correct answer to choose from, so don't write down everything you understand. Just answer the question.

Daily routine

In the morning

14 Read about these people's routines.

Jonas — Ich stehe um sechs Uhr auf.   **Alex** — Um Viertel vor acht frühstücke ich.

David — Ich bade um acht Uhr.   **Claudia** — Um halb acht putze ich mir die Zähne.

Gabi — Um zehn vor acht fahre ich mit dem Bus in die Schule.

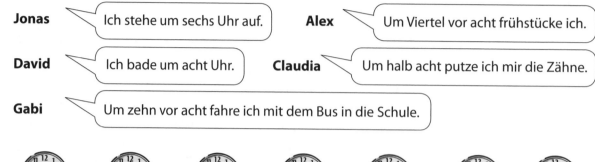

| A | B | C | D | E | F | G |

| 1 | 2 | 3 | 4 | 5 | 6 | 7 |

What activity do people do when? Write the correct letters and numbers in the boxes.

	Time	Activity
Example: Jonas	G	7
(a) Alex		
(b) David		
(c) Claudia		
(d) Gabi		

(2 marks)
(2 marks)
(2 marks)
(2 marks)

A change to school routine

15 Listen to Herr Bach being interviewed on local radio about a proposed change to the school day. Make notes in English in the grid.

(a)

(i) Pupils' complaint:	*(1 mark)*
(ii) A quarter of pupils:	*(1 mark)*
(iii) Weekend advantage:	*(1 mark)*
(iv) Pupils' demand:	*(1 mark)*

(b)

(i) Teachers' suggestion:	*(1 mark)*
(ii) Herr Bach's opinion:	*(1 mark)*

Breakfast

Breakfast choices

16 These people are talking about what they have for breakfast.

Peter Zum Frühstück essen wir zu Hause immer Brot mit Käse. Ich trinke Fruchtsaft.

Kai Ich esse meistens Toastbrot mit Marmelade und ich trinke dazu heiße Schokolade. Ich trinke nie Kaffee oder Tee.

Amir Ich esse mein Frühstück im Schulbus! Mein Lieblingsessen ist Brötchen mit Schinken. Ich trinke dazu eine Cola.

Angela Zum Frühstück esse ich immer ein Stück Obst, wie zum Beispiel einen Apfel oder eine Banane. Ich trinke nichts dazu.

Olivia Ich esse ein Spiegelei mit Toastbrot zum Frühstück. Ich trinke manchmal eine Tasse Tee dazu, wenn ich noch Zeit habe.

FOOD

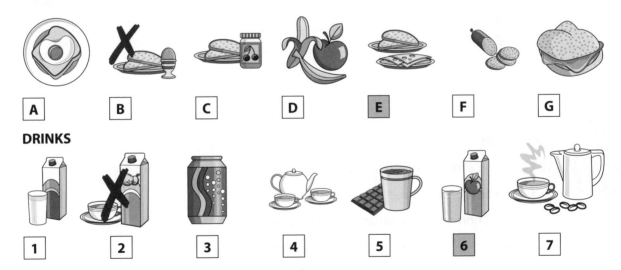

| A | B | C | D | E | F | G |

DRINKS

| 1 | 2 | 3 | 4 | 5 | 6 | 7 |

Write the correct letters and numbers in the boxes.

	Eats	Drinks	
Example: Peter	E	6	
(a) Kai			*(2 marks)*
(b) Amir			*(2 marks)*
(c) Angela			*(2 marks)*
(d) Olivia			*(2 marks)*

Eating at home

Meals at home

17 You read an article about eating at home.

>
> **Tom (15):**
>
> Das Frühstück ist zu Hause oft sehr stressig, weil wir nicht viel Zeit haben. Wir essen oft schnell nur ein Toastbrot und trinken ein Glas Milch oder Fruchtsaft.
>
> Das Abendessen ist viel ruhiger. Wir essen in der Woche um achtzehn Uhr und am Wochenende um neunzehn Uhr.
>
> Es gibt ziemlich oft Nudeln, weil die ganze Familie sie mag. Man kann Nudeln ganz schnell zubereiten. Wir essen nicht gern Reis. Mein Lieblingsessen ist Schweinekotelett mit Kartoffeln. Das ist lecker. Mein Bruder liebt Bratwurst mit Gemüse, aber er mag keine Kartoffeln. Ich esse nicht gern Omelett oder Salat.

Write the correct letter in the box.

(a) Tom thinks breakfast is often …

A	relaxed
B	late
C	rushed

☐ *(1 mark)*

(b) During the week, dinner is at …

A	16:00
B	18:00
C	19:00

☐ *(1 mark)*

(c) Everyone in the family likes …

A	pasta
B	rice
C	potatoes

☐ *(1 mark)*

(d) Tom's favourite meal is …

A	sausage with vegetables
B	pork with potatoes
C	omelette with salad

☐ *(1 mark)*

Laura's visit

18 Listen to Laura describing a visit to her cousin. Which **two** statements are correct?

(a) Write the **two** correct letters in the boxes.

  A I normally ate ham and bread for breakfast.

  B I didn't enjoy the cake as it had cream on it.

  C I loved the cake but I didn't have any cream with it.

  D I normally ate fruit for breakfast.   ☐ ☐ *(2 marks)*

(b) Write the **two** correct letters in the boxes.

  A My cousin doesn't like meat.

  B My favourite food is sausages and potatoes.

  C My cousin doesn't like chicken.

  D My favourite drink is coffee.   ☐ ☐ *(2 marks)*

Eating in a café

Café orders

19 Julia has noted down the meal order for table 7.

Café am Museum

Tisch 7:

Pommes frites

Schaschlik

Eis

Fruchtsaft

Mineralwasser

What did the customer order? Write the four correct letters in the boxes.

Example: A ☐ ☐ ☐ ☐

(4 marks)

Ordering food and drink

20 Listen to the customers in the café. What do they order?

A	Omelette		F	Hamburger
B	Chips		G	Milk
C	Sausage		H	Lemonade
D	Ice cream		I	Fruit juice
E	Kebab			

Write the correct letter in the box.

Example: A

(a) ☐   *(1 mark)*

(b) ☐   *(1 mark)*

(c) ☐   *(1 mark)*

(d) ☐   *(1 mark)*

(e) ☐   *(1 mark)*

(f) ☐   *(1 mark)*

Eating in a restaurant

Family meals out

21 Read Hanna's blog.

> Einmal im Monat geht die ganze Familie ins Restaurant. Wir machen das sehr gerne.
>
> Normalerweise gehen wir in ein kleines Restaurant in der Nähe, das wir alle lieben. Die Kellner sind sehr freundlich und das Essen ist fantastisch.
>
> Es gibt verschiedene Spezialitäten aus vielen Ländern, aber ich liebe Schnitzel mit Kartoffeln und Salat. Meine Mutter ist Vegetarierin und isst oft Pasta mit einer leckeren Tomatensoße. Wir essen keine Vorspeise, aber wir bestellen immer einen Nachtisch! Die Schokoladentorte ist besonders gut!

Read the following sentences. For each sentence, write **T** (True), **F** (False) or **?** (Not in the text) in the box.

(a) The restaurant is quite far away. ☐ *(1 mark)*

(b) The waiters are young. ☐ *(1 mark)*

(c) The food is quite good. ☐ *(1 mark)*

(d) They serve food from different countries. ☐ *(1 mark)*

(e) Hanna always drinks mineral water with her meal. ☐ *(1 mark)*

(f) Hanna's mother doesn't eat meat. ☐ *(1 mark)*

(g) They always have a starter. ☐ *(1 mark)*

(h) Hanna likes the chocolate gateau. ☐ *(1 mark)*

(i) The restaurant is expensive. ☐ *(1 mark)*

Eating out

22 Listen to Klara talking about her restaurant experiences.

What does she find positive and what does she find negative about eating out?

Positive:
Example: ......She likes eating in restaurants...
(a) Most important:
.... *(1 mark)*
(b) Negative:
(i) .... *(1 mark)*
(ii) .... *(1 mark)*

> You will hear more than two negative points mentioned in the recording, but you only need to write two down in the spaces provided. Don't write any more as they will not be looked at.

Healthy eating

Healthy eating

23 You read this article about healthy eating on the internet.

Wie isst du gesund?

Ben: Als ich jünger war, aß ich zu viele Süßigkeiten und ich trank immer mit meinen Freunden große Flaschen Cola. Jetzt trinken wir täglich zusammen Bier. Als Kind hatte ich riesige Probleme mit den Zähnen. Meiner Meinung nach ist es langweilig, immer nur gesund zu essen. Meine Schwester ist Vegetarierin, aber ihr Essen finde ich schrecklich. Ich esse lieber Hamburger und Pommes. Ich sollte wohl einige Kilos abnehmen, aber ich liebe mein Essen und ich mache nicht gern Diät. Nächstes Jahr werde ich auf die Uni gehen – hoffentlich gibt es dort eine gute Kantine!

Mina: Zu Hause koche ich meistens leckere und gesunde Mahlzeiten ohne viel Salz oder Fett. Mein Lieblingsessen ist Schweinebraten mit Salat. Ich trinke viel Wasser und ich esse immer gesund, weil ich an der Uni Sport studiere. Seit der Gesamtschule esse ich keine Bonbons oder Schokolade – Mensch, habe ich die früher gern gegessen! Wir trainieren viermal in der Woche und ich darf nur einmal in der Woche Alkohol trinken. Und dann nur ein kleines Glas! Wenn man Sportlerin sein möchte, muss man gesund essen, weil man sonst viele Kilos zunehmen würde und das wäre eine Katastrophe für mein Trainingsprogramm.

Who do the following statements apply to?

If the statement applies only to Ben write **B**.

If the statement applies only to Mina write **M**.

If the statement applies to both Ben and Mina write **B + M**.

Example: I cook healthy food. | M |

(a) I am not a vegetarian. ☐ *(1 mark)*   **(e)** I had a sweet tooth when I was young. ☐ *(1 mark)*

(b) I don't drink alcohol often. ☐ *(1 mark)*   **(f)** I am at university. ☐ *(1 mark)*

(c) I need to lose weight. ☐ *(1 mark)*

(d) I have never been healthy. ☐ *(1 mark)*

Young people's eating habits

24 Listen to the doctor being interviewed on the radio. Complete the table.

(a) **(i)** Who does the doctor criticise?	*(1 mark)*
(ii) Why?	*(1 mark)*
(b) What is wrong with fast food places?	*(1 mark)*
(c) What diet does the doctor recommend?	*(1 mark)*
(d) Which food should not be missing from a healthy diet?	*(1 mark)*
(e) What restrictions does the doctor put on pasta?	*(1 mark)*

Health issues

Illness

25 These people have various things wrong with them.

Emil	Ich habe Kopfschmerzen.
Beate	Ich habe Rückenschmerzen.
Maya	Ich bin so müde. Nachts schlafe ich nicht.
Peter	Jetzt tun meine Beine weh.
Florian	Ich habe starke Magenschmerzen.
Tobias	Ich bleibe zu Hause. Ich habe Halsschmerzen.
Laura	Ich bin so durstig – wo ist mein Mineralwasser?

What is the problem? Write the initial of the person: **E** (Emil), **B** (Beate), etc. in the box.

Example: Who is thirsty?   L

Who …

(a) has a headache?   ☐   *(1 mark)*

(b) can't sleep?   ☐   *(1 mark)*

Focus on the key words to help you identify the answers here – you don't need to understand every word in the texts.

(c) has a sore throat?   ☐   *(1 mark)*

(d) has stomach ache?   ☐   *(1 mark)*

At the doctor's

26 What is wrong with these people?

A   B   C   D   E

Listen and write the correct letter in the box.

(a) ☐   *(1 mark)*

(b) ☐   *(1 mark)*

(c) ☐   *(1 mark)*

Look at the pictures before you listen and remind yourself of the German expression for each one.

Health problems

Addictions

27 You read an article about addiction.

> Man ☐ I ☐ nach allem süchtig werden … nach Alkohol, Zigaretten, Handys und sogar nach ☐ . Unten schreiben unsere Leser über ihre Erlebnisse mit der Sucht …
>
> • Mit dreizehn Jahren habe ich meine erste Zigarette geraucht, und seit damals konnte ich nicht damit aufhören. Mit der Zeit ist meine ☐ immer schlechter geworden und ich musste oft deswegen zum Arzt gehen …
>
> • Als junger Mann habe ich oft zu viel ☐ . Ich war eigentlich Alkoholiker und ich musste jeden Tag Bier oder Wein trinken …
>
> • An der Schule war ich total von meinem Handy abhängig. Wenn ich es nicht dabei hatte, wurde ich launisch und ☐ …

Fill in the gaps in the text with words from the table. Write the correct letter in the box.

A	freundlich
B	getrunken
C	Schokolade
D	Zigarette
E	Alkoholismus
F	trinken
G	Gesundheit
H	böse
I	kann

(4 marks)

Karl's grandparents

28 Listen to Karl describing a visit to his grandparents.

(a) What is Karl's opinion of visiting his grandparents?

.... *(1 mark)*

(b) Why does he feel like this?

.... *(1 mark)*

(c) Why does he like to go to the park after lunch?

.... *(1 mark)*

(d) What does his grandfather order to drink at the café?

.... *(1 mark)*

(e) What fact does Karl mention which has helped his grandfather's health?

.... *(1 mark)*

Future relationship plans

Future plans

29 You read three people's views on marriage.

> *Xavier:* In Zukunft möchte ich heiraten, aber im Moment bin ich sehr zufrieden, ledig zu sein. Ich bin noch jung und ich möchte um die Welt reisen und neue Leute kennenlernen. Wenn ich wieder nach Hause komme, werde ich eine Partnerin suchen, aber erst dann!
>
> *Annemarie:* Ich habe keine Lust, einen Mann zu finden! Meine Eltern haben sich scheiden lassen, als ich und meine Schwester noch an der Grundschule waren, und ich fand das schrecklich. Ich besuchte meinen Vater jedes Wochenende, aber ich weine noch heute darüber, dass er nicht bei uns zu Hause geblieben ist.
>
> *Lena:* Seit der Schule habe ich einen festen Freund, den ich liebe. Am letzten Tag der Schule hat er mir einen Verlobungsring gegeben und sobald wir beide mit dem Studium fertig sind, werden wir heiraten und Kinder haben.

Write the initial of the person: **X** (Xavier), **A** (Annemarie) or **L** (Lena) in the box.

Who …

(a) doesn't want to get married? ☐ *(1 mark)*

(b) is in a long-term relationship? ☐ *(1 mark)*

(c) is still upset about their childhood? ☐ *(1 mark)*

(d) is happily single? ☐ *(1 mark)*

(e) wants to have children? ☐ *(1 mark)*

(f) wants to meet lots of people? ☐ *(1 mark)*

Relationships

30 Listen to these people describing their relationship status.

A	Married
B	Engaged
C	Happily single
D	Divorced
E	Looking for a partner
F	Separated

Which word above best describes the people? Write the correct letter in the box.

(a) ☐ *(1 mark)*

(b) ☐ *(1 mark)*

(c) ☐ *(1 mark)*

(d) ☐ *(1 mark)*

Social issues

Voluntary work

31 You read an article in the newspaper about voluntary work.

> Seitdem sein bester Freund obdachlos geworden ist, arbeitet Thomas bei einer Organisation, die bedürftigen Menschen in Dortmund hilft. Dreimal in der Woche arbeitet er freiwillig im Stadtzentrum, wo die Organisation eine Suppenküche für arme Einwohner organisiert. Alle Mitarbeiter sind Freiwillige und helfen aus verschiedenen Gründen, aber sie haben Folgendes gemeinsam: Sie wollen alle diesen Leuten aus der Armut helfen.
>
> Die Kantine ist täglich von zwanzig Uhr bis Mitternacht geöffnet und viele Menschen – Männer sowie Frauen, jung sowie alt – kommen dahin, um ein warmes Essen zu bekommen und mit anderen Leuten zu plaudern. Das Leben auf der Straße ist sehr einsam, und viele Leute finden die Kantine sehr wichtig. In der Kantine gibt es auch immer einen Krankenpfleger, mit dem die Besucher über ihre Sorgen sprechen können und Rat bekommen.
>
> Wenn die Besucher in einem warmen Bett übernachten wollen, schickt man sie mit dem Bus in ein Hotel am Stadtrand, wo sie sicher schlafen und auch duschen können, bevor sie am folgenden Morgen wieder zurück auf die Straße müssen.

(a) What led Thomas to volunteer with this particular organisation?

.... *(1 mark)*

(b) What do all the volunteers have in common?

.... *(1 mark)*

(c) What role, other than providing food, does the canteen provide?

.... *(1 mark)*

(d) Mention one specific type of professional help offered at the centre.

.... *(1 mark)*

(e) What is the drawback of the guest house?

.... *(1 mark)*

Hanna's life story

32 Listen to Hanna talking about her experiences.

(a) Which **two** of these statements express what Hanna says?

    A Hanna has a nice flat.

    B Hanna used to work for a big company.

    C Hanna lived on the street for two years.

    D Hanna had good job prospects.

Write the **two** correct letters in the boxes. ☐ ☐   *(2 marks)*

(b) Which **two** of these statements express what Hanna says?

    A Hanna read about the canteen in a newspaper.

    B Hanna was enthusiastic about the canteen from the start.

    C The canteen helped her to turn her life around.

    D Hanna is no longer homeless.

Write the **two** correct letters in the boxes. ☐ ☐   *(2 marks)*

Social problems

B Social problems

33 Complete each of the following newspaper extracts with one of the words which follow.

Write the correct letter in the box.

Example: Im Sudan gibt es eine Hungersnot – bitte **B** Sie Ihr Geld und helfen Sie diesen armen Leuten, die nichts haben.

A	verlieren
B	**spenden**
C	verdienen

(a) Der Vandalismus in der Gegend wurde immer schlimmer, seitdem eine neue Familie in den Wohnblock eingezogen ist. Ich finde es unglaublich, dass Leute so ☐ sein können.

A	freundlich
B	dankbar
C	gemein

(1 mark)

(b) Da unsere Gesellschaft immer älter wird, müssen Frauen oft gleichzeitig für ihre Eltern und ihre Kinder sorgen. Das führt zu großem Stress in der Familie, weil die Mutter oft auch zur Arbeit gehen muss, um ihre Familie finanziell zu ☐ .

A	unterstützen
B	unterbringen
C	vermeiden

(1 mark)

(c) Die Rassenprobleme der siebziger Jahren waren total anders als die heutigen Probleme in unserer multikulturellen Gesellschaft. Trotzdem sind wir alle verantwortlich, die Lebenschancen aller ☐ zu verbessern.

A	Einwanderer
B	Obdachlosen
C	Arbeitslosen

(1 mark)

(d) Letzten Monat gab es ein schreckliches Verbrechen in unserer Gegend, als zwei Männer ins Haus eines alten Nachbarn eingebrochen sind. Das ☐ , Herr Aunitzky, ist seitdem nicht aus dem Haus gegangen, weil er solche Angst hat.

A	Auskommen
B	Problem
C	Opfer

(1 mark)

B Karl's story

34 Listen to the radio report about a pensioner, Karl. Select **three** statements that sum up what we learn about Karl.

A Karl moved to Zell am See to be closer to his family.

B Karl has two children.

C Karl's wife died of a heart attack.

D Karl enjoys good health.

E Karl used to work overseas.

F Karl's granddaughter will probably move away from Zell am See.

Write the **three** correct letters in the boxes.   ☐ ☐ ☐   *(3 marks)*

General hobbies

Hobbies

1   Adam has written his activities on the calendar to help him keep track of them.

> **Mein Wochenplan für Juli**
>
> **Montag**
> Klavierstunde um 7 Uhr.
>
> **Dienstag**
> Ich koche das Abendessen.
>
> **Mittwoch**
> Ich gehe mit Fabian kegeln.
>
> **Donnerstag**
> Ich spiele mit Opi Schach.
>
> **Freitag**
> Ich gehe abends mit Freunden ins Kino.
>
> **Samstag**
> Jeden Samstag gehe ich schwimmen.
>
> **Sonnstag**
> Abends sehe ich gern fern.

Write the correct letter in the box.

Example: Which month is it?

A	June
B	**July**
C	August

B

(a) What does Adam do on Wednesdays?

A	Guitar
B	Bowling
C	TV

☐   *(1 mark)*

(b) What does Adam do with his grandfather?

A	Play chess
B	Go to the cinema
C	Cook

☐   *(1 mark)*

(c) Which day does Adam have a piano lesson?

A	Tuesday
B	Thursday
C	Monday

☐   *(1 mark)*

(d) What does Adam do on Saturdays?

A	Swim
B	Cycle
C	Homework

☐   *(1 mark)*

Young people and hobbies

2   Listen to these people talking about their hobbies.

    Example: What is Mohammed's hobby? .... listening to music ....

    (a) What is Fiona's hobby?

    .... *(1 mark)*

    (b) What is Max's hobby?

    .... *(1 mark)*

    (c) What is Brigitte's hobby?

    .... *(1 mark)*

    (d) What is Stefan's hobby?

    .... *(1 mark)*

19

Had a go ☐ **Nearly there** ☐ **Nailed it!** ☐

Sport

Sporting activities

3 Which sport do these people enjoy?

Peter ◁ Ich gehe gern kegeln.

Anna ◁ Ich gehe gern schwimmen, besonders im Freibad.

Christine ◁ Ich spiele jede Woche Fußball.

Paul ◁ Ich mache gern Leichtathletik, aber das ist ziemlich anstrengend.

Gabi ◁ Ich finde Reiten fantastisch.

Ivor ◁ Im Winter fahre ich gern Schlittschuh.

Kai ◁ Im Winter fahre ich immer mit der Schule Ski.

| A | B | C | D | E | F | G | H | I |

Complete the table by writing the correct letter.

Example: Peter	F	*(1 mark)*
Christine		*(1 mark)*
Gabi		*(1 mark)*
Ivor		*(1 mark)*
Anna		*(1 mark)*
Paul		*(1 mark)*
Kai		*(1 mark)*

> If you find the vocabulary from the sentences that matches the picture, you have found the correct answer.

Sporting opinions

4 Listen to Georg, Julia and Thomas discussing sport.

What do they say?

A	'I have never played for a team.'
B	'I enjoy training hard.'
C	'I had to swap football for table tennis.'
D	'I have never tried table tennis.'
E	'I find training tiring.'

Write the correct letter in the box.

(a) George ☐   *(1 mark)*

(b) Julia ☐   *(1 mark)*

(c) Thomas ☐   *(1 mark)*

Arranging to go out

An invitation to the cinema

5   Salma has invited her friends to go to the cinema. Here are their replies.

A

Ich kann nicht ins Kino gehen, weil ich Kopfschmerzen habe. Ich muss zu Hause bleiben. Ich schicke dir eine SMS, wenn es mir besser geht.

C

Ich möchte lieber einen Liebesfilm sehen, aber wenn du die Eintrittskarten kaufst, komme ich vielleicht doch mit!

E

Am Samstag bin ich in Frankfurt, weil ich dort Hockey spiele. Wir kommen erst um 10 Uhr abends mit dem Zug nach Hause zurück.

B

Toll! Ich komme mit! Aber ich muss zuerst meine Oma besuchen. Wann beginnt die Vorstellung?

D

Ich habe den Film schon letzte Woche gesehen. Er war gut, aber ich will ihn nicht zweimal sehen. Möchtest du nicht lieber in den Skatepark gehen?

F

Ach, das ist schade. Ich gehe auf die Hochzeit meiner Tante und wir feiern sicher bis spät in die Nacht. Nächstes Mal komme ich aber mit, weil ich sehr gern ins Kino gehe.

Write the correct letter in the box.

Who...

(a) has already seen the film?	☐	*(1 mark)*
(b) would rather see a romantic film?	☐	*(1 mark)*
(c) is not feeling well?	☐	*(1 mark)*
(d) wants to know the time of the film?	☐	*(1 mark)*
(e) will see the film if Salma buys the tickets?	☐	*(1 mark)*
(f) will not be back in time?	☐	*(1 mark)*
(g) will text Salma?	☐	*(1 mark)*

> Be careful! The same person might be the answer more than once.

Going out

6   Listen to Demi talking about an invitation she has received from a friend.

Write the correct letter in the box.

(a) What has her mum told her she can't do?

A	Go to the concert
B	Stay out after 10 o'clock
C	Get to the cinema late

☐   *(1 mark)*

(b) Why can't she go on Tuesday evening?

A	She has Maths tuition
B	She has to revise for a test
C	She is never free on Tuesdays

☐   *(1 mark)*

(c) What should she and her friend do?

A	Book the tickets now
B	Get to the cinema at 7 o'clock
C	Take 3D glasses with them

☐   *(1 mark)*

(d) What time will they meet?

A	Half past seven
B	Seven o'clock
C	Quarter past seven

☐   *(1 mark)*

What I did last weekend

B

An active weekend

7 Jusuf has written a blog about last weekend.

> Normalerweise mache ich am Wochenende nicht viel, weil ich viele Schularbeiten habe. Aber letztes Wochenende hatte ich ein wunderbares Erlebnis, das ich nie vergessen werde.
>
> Weil mein Freund Peter Geburtstag hatte, sind wir am Samstag ganz früh ins neue Freizeitzentrum außerhalb der Stadt gefahren, wo man viele tolle Aktivitäten machen kann. Peters Vater hat die Eintrittskarten im Voraus gekauft und es war für Peter eine große Überraschung. Er hatte geglaubt, dass wir zu seinen Großeltern an der Küste fahren würden. Als Erstes sind wir beide reiten gegangen und ich fand das toll, obwohl es mein erstes Mal auf einem Pferd war. Peter kann sehr gut reiten und es hat ihm besonders Spaß gemacht. Er hat mich ein bisschen ausgelacht, weil ich ziemlich nervös war.
>
> Am Nachmittag sind wir beide in den Wald nebenan gegangen, wo man schön klettern kann. Klettern ist mein Lieblingshobby und für mich war es ziemlich einfach, aber Peter musste viel Neues lernen, und da es ziemlich windig war, hatte er Angst.

Read the following sentences. Write **T** (True), **F** (False) or **?** (Not in the text) in the box.

(a) At the weekend Jusuf usually does his homework. ☐ *(1 mark)*

(b) Last weekend something amazing happened. ☐ *(1 mark)*

(c) His friend Peter was celebrating his 16th birthday. ☐ *(1 mark)*

(d) Jusuf had to buy his own ticket. ☐ *(1 mark)*

(e) Peter was expecting to visit his grandparents. ☐ *(1 mark)*

(f) Jusuf likes horses. ☐ *(1 mark)*

(g) Jusuf and Peter were not evenly matched at riding or climbing. ☐ *(1 mark)*

(h) Peter was worried it might be windy. ☐ *(1 mark)*

> The answer can only be True (**T**) if it is stated in the text or False (**F**) if the opposite is stated in the text – otherwise the answer will be Not in the text (**?**).

B

Last weekend

8 Listen to Thomas describing what he did last weekend.

What did he think of the activities?

Write **P** for positive. Write **N** for negative.

Write **P + N** for positive and negative.

(a) Swimming ☐ *(1 mark)*   **(c)** Invitation to party ☐ *(1 mark)*

(b) Bus journey ☐ *(1 mark)*   **(d)** Party activities ☐ *(1 mark)*

TV programmes

Mehmet's TV texts

9 Mehmet has been texting his friend about TV.

- Viele Seifenopern sind langweilig. Ich sehe mir **A** Sportsendungen an.
- Mittwochs gibt es einen tollen Krimi. Das sehe ich mir jede ☐ an.
- Die besten Sendungen, finde ich, sind Komödien. Ich ☐ die ganze Zeit und das ärgert meine Schwester!
- Jeden Nachmittag sieht mein kleiner Bruder einen ☐ oder eine Kindersendung, aber ich finde sie blöd.
- Auch die Werbung geht mir auf die Nerven und meiner Meinung nach soll man sie nicht ☐ !

Fill the gaps with a word from the list below. Write the correct letter in the box.

A	lieber
B	lache
C	zeigen
D	Woche
E	Horrorfilm
F	sehen
G	langweile mich
H	Wochenende
I	Zeichentrickfilm

> Remember to read carefully either side of the gap to get as many clues as possible to the answer.

(4 marks)

Television

10 Listen to these teenagers talking about TV programmes they watch.

What do they think of the programmes?

Write **P** for positive.

Write **N** for negative.

Write **P + N** for positive and negative.

(a) ☐ *(1 mark)*

(b) ☐ *(1 mark)*

(c) ☐ *(1 mark)*

(d) ☐ *(1 mark)*

23

Cinema

A German film

11 Fill the gaps with a word from the list below. Write the correct letter in the box.

(a) Im deutschen Abenteuerfilm „Yoko" ging es um die ☐ zwischen einem Yeti, Yoko, der in den Bergen des Himalajas wohnt, und einem deutschen Mädchen, Pia. Eines Tages kommt Yoko nach Deutschland, wo Pia ihn kennenlernt.

A	Trennung
B	Freundschaft
C	Streit

(1 mark)

(b) Meine Schwester geht nie ins Kino, weil sie das als eine Geldverschwendung betrachtet. Sie meint, es ist viel günstiger, Videos aus dem Internet herunterzuladen, aber das würde ich nie machen, weil das gesetzlich ☐ ist.

A	verboten
B	erlaubt
C	teuer

(1 mark)

(c) Letzte Woche habe ich im Stadtkino einen französischen Film gesehen und die Geschichte hat mir recht gut gefallen, weil sie sehr lustig und spannend war. Obwohl es auch schöne Effekte und tolle Musik gab, habe ich mich wegen der ☐ im Film geärgert.

A	Lieder
B	Untertitel
C	Handlung

(1 mark)

(d) Gestern wollte ich unbedingt ins Kino gehen, um den neuesten Kinofilm in der Reihe „Blaue Band" zu sehen, aber man musste dafür stundenlang Schlange stehen und ich kann das nicht leiden. Ich bin also ☐ nach Hause gefahren, ohne den Film gesehen zu haben.

A	hoffnungsvoll
B	überrascht
C	enttäuscht

(1 mark)

> Eliminate the answer options you know to be wrong first.

A trip to the cinema

12 Listen to Alfred describing a trip to the cinema. Write the correct letter in the box.

(a) Why did Albert choose this film?

A	He had read a good review.
B	Romantic films are his favourite.
C	His cousin recommended it.

☐

(1 mark)

(b) What annoyed Alfred about the film?

A	It wasn't funny.
B	It made him cry.
C	The lead actress.

☐

(1 mark)

(c) Why did Alfred go on Wednesday?

A	His friend was available then.
B	There was a good deal available.
C	A premier seat was available for €11.

☐

(1 mark)

> Don't jump to conclusions – listen to the whole of the recording.

Music

D

A German band

13 You read this article about **Juli**, a German Band.

Juli ist eine Pop-Rock-Band aus Gießen in der Nähe von Frankfurt, Deutschland. Ihre erste Single „Perfekte Welle" war 2004 auf Platz Nummer 2 der deutschen Musikcharts. 2006 war ihr Album „Ein neuer Tag" auf Nummer 1.

Eva Briegel (Sängerin) schreibt gemeinsam mit Simon Triebel und Jonas Pfetzing (Gitarre) die Lieder auf Deutsch. Man hört ihre Musik sehr oft im deutschen Radio.

Which **four** sentences are correct?

A	The band is called **Juli**.
B	The band is from a town close to Frankfurt.
C	Their album *A new day* was a success.
D	They released their first single in 2006.
E	Eva plays the guitar.
F	Their songs are in English.
G	The group write their own lyrics.
H	There are four members in the band.
I	The band is often played on German radio.

Write the **four** correct letters in the boxes.

Example: A ☐ ☐ ☐ ☐   *(4 marks)*

B

Music

14 Listen to Elias, Charlotte and Leon talking about music. What do they think?

A	'I can't bear waiting till the end of the year to hear music again.'
B	'The concert was a waste of time.'
C	'My parents can't afford for me to have any music lessons.'
D	'I am going to buy an MP3-player.'
E	'I will be cross if the band don't play again.'
F	'I think music is an important aspect of life.'

Write the correct letter in the box.

(a) Elias   ☐   *(1 mark)*   **(c)** Leon   ☐   *(1 mark)*

(b) Charlotte   ☐   *(1 mark)*

New technology

A

The internet

15 You read this article about the internet.

> **Markus (16)** sucht oft Informationen für die Schularbeiten im Internet, weil ihm das schnell bei vielen Aufgaben hilft. Seine Eltern sind froh, dass er die Hausaufgaben selbstständig machen kann, weil sie ihm nicht dabei helfen können. Bis spät in die Nacht benutzt Markus aber auch seinen Tablet-PC, um stundenlang mit Freunden zu chatten und sich Videoclips anzusehen. Darüber machen sich seine Eltern Sorgen, weil sie selber nicht mit dem Internet zurechtkommen und sie meinen, dass es gefährlich für ihren Sohn sein könnte, weil sie so etwas in der Zeitung gelesen haben.
>
> **Meryem (19)** sucht online Informationen über Filme. Sie findet es praktisch, weil man schnell sehen kann, welche Filme laufen und ob man sie empfehlen würde. Ab und zu kaufen sie und ihre Mutter auch Kleidung im Internet, aber letzten Monat hat ihre Mutter ein neues Kleid bestellt und dafür mit der Kreditkarte bezahlt. Leider ist das Kleid nie mit der Post angekommen und das Geld ist von ihrem Konto verschwunden. Jetzt geht sie wieder lieber ins Einkaufszentrum, weil sie glaubt, dass das Internet gefährlich ist.

(a) Why is it important that Markus can do his homework independently?

.... *(1 mark)*

(b) Why wouldn't Markus's parents be able to research films online?

.... *(1 mark)*

(c) What attitude do Markus's parents and Meryem's mother share about the internet?

.... *(1 mark)*

(d) Why does Meryem particularly like researching films online? Mention one reason.

.... *(1 mark)*

(e) What changed Meryem's mother's attitude towards the internet?

.... *(1 mark)*

E

Young people and the internet

16 Listen to these people talking about the internet.

What do they use the internet for?

Example: ...writing emails...

(a) .... *(1 mark)*

(b) .... *(1 mark)*

(c) .... *(1 mark)*

(d) .... *(1 mark)*

> Learn plenty of basic vocabulary before the exam so you can answer questions like these without too much trouble.

Language of the internet

Information technology

17 You read these adverts at the internet café.

A 1000 zufriedene Benutzer besuchen täglich unsere Webseite. Schauen Sie mal hin!	**E** Wir speichern Ihre Bilder und Videos! Sie können Lieder, Videos und Sendungen jetzt hochladen und bei uns speichern.
B Funktioniert Ihr Computer nicht? Ist er langsam und veraltet? Rufen Sie uns heute an ...	**F** Brauchen Sie Hilfe beim Interneteinkaufen? Wir sind da, um Ihnen zu helfen!
C Schützen Sie Ihre Technologie vom neuesten Virus mit unserem Software.	**G** Jede Minute kommt ein neues Lied zum Herunterladen bei uns an!
D Vergessen Sie immer Ihre Passwörter? Als Computerprogrammierer kann ich Ihnen bei diesem Problem helfen.	

Write the correct letter in the box.

Example: Who can help with storage problems?   `E`

(a) Who claims to have lots of satisfied users?   ☐   *(1 mark)*

(b) Where can you go to download music?   ☐   *(1 mark)*

(c) Who can help you to improve your computer?   ☐   *(1 mark)*

(d) Who can help you with shopping?   ☐   *(1 mark)*

Working with new technology

18 Listen to Carola talking about her job.

  (a) (i) Why does Carola have to go abroad?

.... *(1 mark)*

     (ii) What is her opinion of her job?

.... *(1 mark)*

     (iii) What would she have to be careful about if she worked from home?

.... *(1 mark)*

  (b) (i) Why is Carola's firm not more forward-thinking?

.... *(1 mark)*

     (ii) Explain the advantage of not working in an office, according to Carola?

.... *(1 mark)*

     (iii) What is Carola planning to do to change things?

.... *(1 mark)*

Internet pros and cons

Pros and cons of the internet

19 Read what these teenagers think about the internet.

> **Max**: Ich vergesse immer mein Passwort. Das ist dumm!
>
> **Tom**: Ich kann meinem Freund in Frankreich problemlos E-Mails schreiben.
>
> **Adam**: Ich finde es sehr nützlich für die Hausaufgaben.
>
> **Lara**: Ich glaube, das Internet kann manchmal gefährlich sein.
>
> **Olivia**: Es gibt viele tolle Webseiten. Ich kann alles online finden.
>
> **Birgit**: Ich chatte online zu viel mit Freunden und meine Eltern finden das nervig!
>
> **Jonas**: Ich spiele jeden Abend online und so langweile ich mich nie!

Who says what? Write the correct initial in the box: **M** for Max, **T** for Tom, etc.

Example: I like playing games online.   [J]

(a) I think the internet can be dangerous.   ☐   *(1 mark)*

(b) I find the internet useful for school work.   ☐   *(1 mark)*

(c) I can keep in touch with my friend.   ☐   *(1 mark)*

(d) I can find everything online.   ☐   *(1 mark)*

> Never leave an answer box blank – answer the ones you are confident of first, then use a process of elimination to make an intelligent guess for any missing answers.

Internet

20 Listen to Markus and Sandra discussing the internet.

(a) (i) What does Markus mostly use the internet for?

.... *(1 mark)*

(ii) How does Sandra get access to the internet?

.... *(1 mark)*

(iii) What problem does Sandra have?

.... *(1 mark)*

(b) (i) What is Markus's solution to the password problem?

.... *(1 mark)*

(ii) What does Sandra think of this solution?

.... *(1 mark)*

(iii) What did Sandra recently read about in the newspaper?

.... *(1 mark)*

(c) (i) Why does Markus's mother have to go abroad?

.... *(1 mark)*

(ii) Exactly when did Sandra get a new mobile phone?

.... *(1 mark)*

Shops

A shopping trip

21 Read Amit's shopping list.

Supermarkt	25,00 €
Post	0,75 €
Bäckerei	5,60 €
Fischgeschäft	7,80 €
Buchhandlung	13,00 €
Parfümerie	30,00 €
Zeitungskiosk	2,50 €

How much did Amit spend at each shop?

Example: Fish shop ..... € ..7,80...........

(a) Supermarket   € .... *(1 mark)*   **(c)** Bookshop   € .... *(1 mark)*

(b) Newspaper kiosk € .... *(1 mark)*   **(d)** Bakery   € .... *(1 mark)*

Where I like to shop

22 Listen to Karola and Benjamin discussing where they like to shop.

(a) **(i)** Where does Karola go if she has to shop?

.... *(1 mark)*

(ii) What advantage does she mention about going there?

.... *(1 mark)*

(iii) Why exactly did she go to the music shop last weekend?

.... *(1 mark)*

(iv) What disadvantage does she mention about the music shop?

.... *(1 mark)*

(b) **(i)** What does Benjamin dislike about department stores?

.... *(1 mark)*

(ii) Why does he go to the smaller shops?

.... *(1 mark)*

(iii) How does he cope with the extra cost of the clothes?

.... *(1 mark)*

(iv) What does he find a pity?

.... *(1 mark)*

> Listen for gist first time round and make notes to help you answer the questions. Your
> second listening will have to be detailed so you can get answers to all the questions.

29

Food shopping

F

Shopping list

23 Miriam has written a shopping list.

Which items does Miriam need to buy?

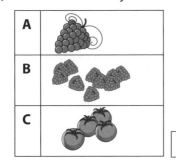

EINKAUFSLISTE

eine Dose Erbsen
ein Glas Himbeermarmelade
eine Tüte Kartoffeln
1 Kilo Rindfleisch
6 Brötchen
2 Liter Vollmilch
1 Kilo Champignons
rote Äpfel
3 Scheiben Schinken
1 Hähnchen

A   B   C

D   E   F

G   H   I

Write the **four** correct letters in the boxes.

Example: A ☐ ☐ ☐ ☐   *(4 marks)*

E

At the grocer

24 Listen to Olivia at the grocer. Write the correct letter in the box.

(a) What does she buy first?

A	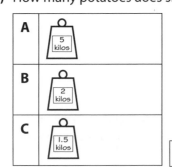
B	
C	

☐ *(1 mark)*

(c) What costs €3.70?

A	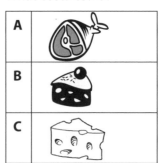
B	
C	

☐ *(1 mark)*

(b) How many potatoes does she buy?

A	5 kilos
B	2 kilos
C	1.5 kilos

☐ *(1 mark)*

(d) What does she buy half a kilo of?

A	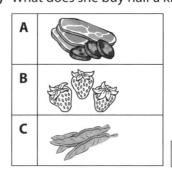
B	
C	

☐ *(1 mark)*

Shopping

Shopping

25 Read Ahmed's blog.

> Ich gehe gern einkaufen. Letzte Woche habe ich im Schaufenster eines Kaufhauses einen tollen MP3-Spieler gesehen. Im Moment spare ich und ich hoffe, ihn nächsten Monat zu kaufen.
>
> Jeden Freitag gehe ich mit meinem Vater in den Supermarkt. Ich finde es nicht zu langweilig, aber letzten Freitag war es furchtbar, weil der Einkaufswagen kaputt war!
>
> Ich kaufe gern Kleidung auf dem Markt, weil es dort oft billiger als im Kaufhaus ist. Letzten Samstag habe ich eine tolle Hose gefunden und sie hat nicht viel gekostet.
>
> Am Wochenende werde ich mit meinem Vater einkaufen gehen, um einen neuen Fernsehapparat auszusuchen.

Read the following sentences. Write **T** (True), **F** (False) or **?** (Not in the text) in the box.

(a) Ahmed saw the MP3-player in the music department. ☐ *(1 mark)*

(b) Ahmed has enough money to buy the player. ☐ *(1 mark)*

(c) Ahmed finds supermarket trips a bit dull. ☐ *(1 mark)*

(d) The trolley was broken. ☐ *(1 mark)*

(e) Supermarket clothes are better quality than the ones in the market. ☐ *(1 mark)*

(f) Ahmed bought a shirt at the market. ☐ *(1 mark)*

(g) Ahmed is going shopping with his dad at the weekend. ☐ *(1 mark)*

(h) They are going to return their TV as it is faulty. ☐ *(1 mark)*

> Words like *weil*, *als*, etc. send the verb to the end of the clause – if you are struggling to understand the sentence, look at the end and find the verb which might help your understanding.

Shopping for shoes

26 Listen to Elias talking about his recent shopping trip.

(a) Why exactly did Elias have to buy new shoes?

.... *(1 mark)*

(b) Why exactly was Elias disappointed at the shopping centre?

.... *(1 mark)*

(c) Name an advantage and a disadvantage at the department store.

Advantage: .... *(1 mark)*

Disadvantage: .... *(1 mark)*

(d) Why exactly could Elias go to the snack bar?

.... *(1 mark)*

> If the question asks 'exactly', you must be precise in your answer and give the detail required. Make sure in the second listening that you have noted enough relevant detail in your answer.

Clothes and colours

F **Clothes shopping**

27 These people are shopping for clothes.

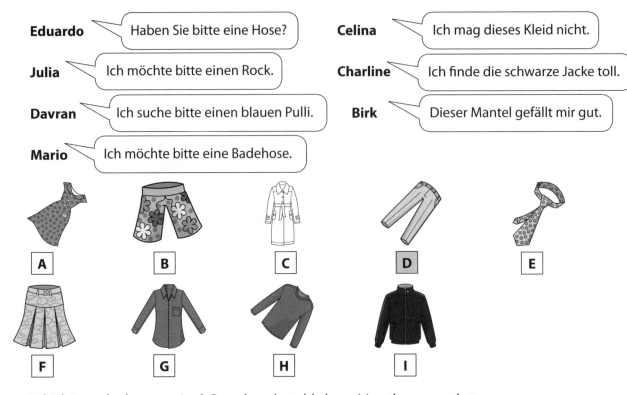

Eduardo — Haben Sie bitte eine Hose?

Julia — Ich möchte bitte einen Rock.

Davran — Ich suche bitte einen blauen Pulli.

Mario — Ich möchte bitte eine Badehose.

Celina — Ich mag dieses Kleid nicht.

Charline — Ich finde die schwarze Jacke toll.

Birk — Dieser Mantel gefällt mir gut.

A   B   C   D   E

F   G   H   I

Which item do they mention? Complete the table by writing the correct letter.

Example: Eduardo	D
Julia		*(1 mark)*
Davran		*(1 mark)*
Mario		*(1 mark)*

Celina		*(1 mark)*
Charline		*(1 mark)*
Birk		*(1 mark)*

G **Buying clothes**

28 What clothes do Ingo and Ulrike buy?

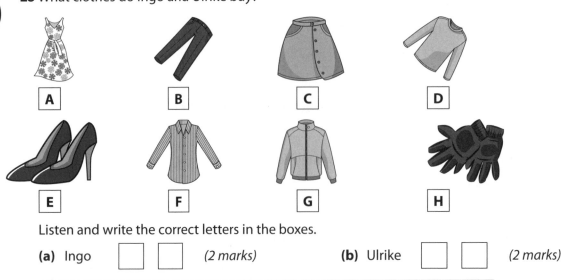

A   B   C   D

E   F   G   H

Listen and write the correct letters in the boxes.

(a) Ingo ☐ ☐ *(2 marks)*   **(b)** Ulrike ☐ ☐ *(2 marks)*

> Look carefully at any pictures before you listen and note the German words for the items you remember – then listen for those words while the recording is played.

Buying clothes

Clothes

29 Read Bärbel's blog about clothes.

> Ich liebe Mode und ich kaufe mir jeden Monat neue Klamotten. Die Farbe ist mir am wichtigsten. Dunkle Farben stehen mir am besten. Gelb und Weiß stehen mir gar nicht. Ich probiere Kleidung lieber zu Hause an, weil die Umkleidekabinen im Laden viel zu eng sind. Wenn sie mir nicht passen, gehe ich in den Laden zurück und ich tausche sie um.
>
> Markenkleidung kaufe ich nur ab und zu, weil sie meistens zu teuer ist. Ich kaufe sehr gern Stiefel und Mützen auf dem Markt, weil sie viel billiger sind.

Write the correct letter in the box.

(a) Which particular colours do not suit Bärbel?

A	Dark colours
B	White and yellow
C	Bright colours

(1 mark)

(b) Where does she try clothes on?

A	She doesn't need to as she can tell if they fit or not
B	In the changing room
C	At home

(1 mark)

(c) How often does she buy designer clothes?

A	Now and again
B	Often
C	Never, as they are too expensive

(1 mark)

(d) What does she buy at the market?

A	Boots and caps
B	Boots and coats
C	Caps and shoes

(1 mark)

Getting the right outfit

30 Listen to Melanie and Sofia buying clothes for a party.

What is **their** opinion of each item?

Write **P** for positive. Write **N** for negative.

Write **P + N** for positive and negative.

(a) Trousers ☐   *(1 mark)*

(b) Jacket ☐   *(1 mark)*

(c) Jumper ☐   *(1 mark)*

(d) Dress ☐   *(1 mark)*

Returning clothes

B

Dissatisfied customers

31 These customers are returning goods they have bought.

Anna — Ich habe letzte Woche die Schuhe gekauft, aber sie passen nicht zum Kleid. Die Farbe ist zu hell und ich möchte sie zurückbringen, wenn möglich.

Marta — Als ich die Strickjacke heute anziehen wollte, habe ich bemerkt, dass sie schmutzig war. Ich habe die Quittung in der Handtasche.

Jens — Ich habe die Hose online gekauft – sie sollte aus Wolle sein, aber sie ist aus Kunststoff und deshalb kann ich sie nicht tragen, weil ich dagegen allergisch bin.

Elke — Obwohl das Kleid sehr schön ist, passt es mir nicht gut. Es ist ein bisschen zu eng und ich hätte das Kleid lieber in der nächsten Größe.

Nils — Die Hose passt mir sehr gut, aber meine Mutter findet sie zu teuer. Ich möchte bitte mein Geld zurück.

Sabine — Ich möchte die Jacke umtauschen, weil sie von schlechter Qualität ist und außerdem ist sie zu warm für den Sommer.

Fabian — Entschuldigung, aber diese Trainingsschuhe sind beschädigt. Bekomme ich bitte mein Geld zurück?

> Sometimes the same person will be the answer to more than one question, so don't rule anyone out just because you have noted them down once.

Write the initial of the person: **A** (Anna), **M** (Marta), etc. Who …

(a) does not like the fabric? ☐

(b) thinks the colour is wrong? ☐

(c) would like a bigger size item? ☐

(d) has bought some damaged shoes? ☐

(e) has an allergy to certain materials? ☐

(f) bought the item a week ago? ☐

(6 marks)

D

Taking an item back

32 Listen to Max returning an item of clothing to the shop. Write the correct letter in the box.

32

(a) Why is Max returning the item?

A	He does not like it
B	It does not fit him
C	It is the wrong colour

☐

(c) Which item of clothing has a 10% reduction?

A	Jumper
B	Trousers
C	Shirt

☐

(b) What is the problem with the other shirts?

A	Max does not like the colours
B	They are more expensive
C	They are a bit short

☐

(d) What is Max's opinion about the exchange?

A	Would have preferred another shirt
B	Feels disappointed
C	Prefers the new item to the shirt

☐

(4 marks)

Shopping opinions

Shopping preferences

33 You read the following article.

Am Wochenende sind die Einkaufszentren und Stadtzentren überfüllt. Einkaufen scheint als Freizeitaktivität beliebter als Joggen oder Schwimmen zu sein.

Jeden Samstag schaut sich Max (16) in den Geschäften in der Stadtmitte um. Er kauft nur ab und zu etwas, aber er findet es toll, sich am Wochenende die neueste Mode anzusehen. Er geht lieber mit Freunden einkaufen. „Ich probiere etwas an. Dann helfen sie mir, wenn ich nicht weiß, ob ich es kaufen soll. Leider bezahlen sie nicht!"

Anna (15) kann Einkaufen nicht leiden. „Einkaufen interessiert mich gar nicht. Ich treibe lieber Sport. Meine Mutter kauft meine Klamotten im Internet. Ich finde das praktisch, weil ich alles zu Hause anprobieren kann. Es ist auch einfach und billiger."

Für Maria (18) ist Mode ihre große Leidenschaft. Sie findet Mode viel besser als Sport oder Musik. „Ich gehe lieber in Boutiquen, weil die Kleidung dort besonders modisch ist. Die Auswahl ist vielleicht nicht so groß wie in größeren Geschäften und Warenhäusern, aber man findet schöne Sachen, die ein bisschen anders und nicht zu teuer sind."

(a) Why are shopping centres so full these days?

.... *(1 mark)*

(b) Mention one positive and one negative aspect of going shopping with friends, according to Max.

  (i) Positive: .... *(1 mark)*

  (ii) Negative: .... *(1 mark)*

(c) Mention one reason why Anna rarely goes shopping for clothes.

.... *(1 mark)*

(d) What is Maria's attitude to clothes shopping?

.... *(1 mark)*

(e) Mention one advantage and one disadvantage of shopping in boutiques, according to Maria.

  (i) Advantage: .... *(1 mark)*

  (ii) Disadvantage: .... *(1 mark)*

Shopping opinions

34 Listen to these teenagers discussing their opinions on shopping.

Write **P** for positive. Write **N** for negative.

Write **P + N** for positive and negative.

> You cannot answer this sort of question until you have heard the whole extract – don't switch your mind off before the end.

(a) [ ]   *(1 mark)*   **(c)** [ ]   *(1 mark)*

(b) [ ]   *(1 mark)*   **(d)** [ ]   *(1 mark)*

Pocket money

Shopping catalogue

35 This catalogue has just been delivered to your home.

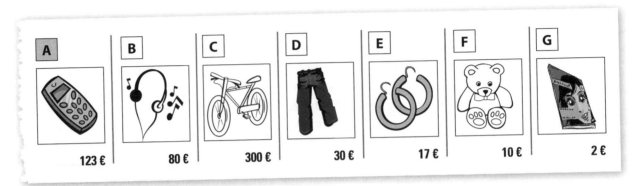

A	B	C	D	E	F	G
123 €	80 €	300 €	30 €	17 €	10 €	2 €

Match the following statements to the items in the catalogue.

Write the sum of money each person needs to save.

Example: Ich spare auf ein Handy, weil mein Handy jetzt sehr altmodisch ist.   123€

(a)   Ich lese sehr gern und bald mache ich eine lange Zugreise mit der Familie.

☐

(1 mark)

(b)   Meine Eltern geben mir dreißig Euro pro Monat – nächste Woche kann ich mir neue Kleidung kaufen.

☐

(1 mark)

(c)   Ich habe keinen Schmuck, der zu meinem Kleid passt und nächsten Monat gehe ich auf ein Fest. Ich muss schnell sparen!

☐

(1 mark)

(d)   Ich spare mein Taschengeld auf der Sparkasse und ich habe fast genug gespart, um mir ein neues Rad zu kaufen.

☐

(1 mark)

Money attitudes

36 Listen to Thomas, Olivia and Tobias talking about their pocket money.

(a) What is Thomas's problem?
.... *(1 mark)*
(b) What is Olivia's attitude to pocket money?
.... *(1 mark)*
(c) What is Tobias's attitude to the money he receives?
.... *(1 mark)*

Holiday destinations

My holiday

37 These people are writing about where they like to stay on holiday.

Ben:	Ich wohne am liebsten in einem Hotel in der Stadtmitte, weil es so viel zu sehen gibt. Letzten Februar waren wir in den Bergen, aber es war schrecklich.
Anna:	Jedes Jahr verbringen wir eine Woche auf einem Bauernhof auf dem Land. Ich finde das gut, weil es dort sehr ruhig ist. Ab und zu besuchen wir auch meine Oma, die in den Bergen wohnt.
Leon:	Normalerweise fahren wir an die Küste und das finde ich perfekt, besonders wenn gutes Wetter ist. Manchmal verbringen wir den Urlaub in einem Dorf, aber das kann total langweilig sein.

Write the initial of the person: **B** (Ben), **A** (Anna), **L** (Leon).

Example: Who sometimes stays in a village?   L

Who …

(a) likes the seaside? ☐ *(1 mark)*

(b) likes the countryside? ☐ *(1 mark)*

(c) hated being in the mountains? ☐ *(1 mark)*

(d) stays on a farm? ☐ *(1 mark)*

> Be careful not to focus on a single word in a sentence, as it could mislead you. You need to understand the context around the key word.

Going on holiday

38 Listen to these teenagers talking about holidays. Where would they like to go?

A

B

C

D

E

F

Write the correct letter in the box.

(a) Almuth ☐ *(1 mark)*   **(c)** Lukas ☐ *(1 mark)*

(b) Viola ☐ *(1 mark)*   **(d)** Lena ☐ *(1 mark)*

Holiday accommodation

Places to stay

39 Read Adam's blog about holiday accommodation.

Jedes Jahr verbringen wir zwei Wochen in Italien. Meine Eltern übernachten am liebsten in einem Hotel. Sie wollen immer ein Zimmer mit Dusche und Balkon, wo sie abends sitzen können. Mein Bruder und ich haben normalerweise ein Zweibettzimmer.

Viele Familien mit kleinen Kindern übernachten gern auf einem Bauernhof. Man kann natürlich im Bauernhaus schlafen, aber oft darf man dort auch zelten oder einen Wohnwagen mieten. Zelten ist billiger und es macht immer viel Spaß, draußen im Freien zu sein.

Jugendherbergen sind toll für junge Leute. Normalerweise sind sie sauber und ziemlich ruhig. Sie sind bequem und haben Zimmer mit WC und Bad oder Dusche. Wenn man alleine reist, kann man oft ein Einzelzimmer buchen.

Which type of accommodation do the following statements apply to?

Write **H** (hotel), **F** (farm) or **Y** (youth hostel) in the box.

Example: This appeals to young travellers.   Y

(a) This appeals to families with young children.	☐	(1 mark)
(b) Adam shares a room with his brother here.	☐	(1 mark)
(c) You can often camp here too.	☐	(1 mark)
(d) The rooms here are comfortable.	☐	(1 mark)
(e) This is the sort of accommodation Adam's parents prefer.	☐	(1 mark)
(f) Single rooms are available here.	☐	(1 mark)

Accommodation

40 Listen to Thomas, Ursula and Alex talking about their holidays.

What did they think of them?

Write **P** for positive.

Write **N** for negative.

Write **P + N** for positive and negative.

(a) Thomas	☐	(1 mark)
(b) Ursula	☐	(1 mark)
(c) Alex	☐	(1 mark)

Booking accommodation

A booking email

41 Max sends an email to the manager of a youth hostel.

```
000                                                         ⬭
  🚫          ↩            ↩↩           ➡          🖨
Löschen   Antworten   Antworten Alle   Weiter    Drucken

Guten Tag!

Im August [        ] ich mit Freunden nach Berlin.

Wir kommen am elften August an und wir möchten drei [        ] bleiben.

Wir sind vier Jungen. Wir möchten bitte, wenn möglich, ein [        ] im
zweiten Stock mit WC und Bad .

Kann man in der Jugendherberge einen [        ] kaufen?

Mit freundlichen Grüßen

Max Seifert
```

Complete the text by using words from the table. Write the correct letter in each box.

A	Reisepass		E	bleibe
B	Familien		F	Nächte
C	fahre		G	Hotel
D	Zimmer		H	Stadtplan

> Don't throw away marks by writing the wrong letter – concentrate all the time!

(4 marks)

At the hotel reception

42 Listen to Luisa at the hotel reception desk.

A	Single room
B	Full-board
C	Breakfast
D	View
E	Swimming pool
F	Double room
G	Gym
H	Telephone

> Look through the words A–H before you listen and remind yourself of the German words for each one.

What does Luisa ask for at reception? Write the **four** correct letters in the boxes.

Example:

A				

(4 marks)

Staying in a hotel

Hotel Advert

43 You see this advert for a hotel.

> Das Hotel steht direkt am Marktplatz, dem Rathaus gegenüber.
>
> *Zimmer:*
>
> Es gibt achtzehn Zimmer (Doppelzimmer, Zweibettzimmer und Einzelzimmer).
>
> Alle Zimmer haben WC und Bad, plus Klimaanlage.
>
> Das Restaurant ist im Erdgeschoss und ist für unsere Gäste täglich von 18 bis 22 Uhr geöffnet.
>
> *Unterhaltung:*
>
> • Jeden Mittwoch ist Kinoabend.
> • Live Sportsendungen kann man im Satellitenfernsehen im Wohnzimmer sehen.
> • Freitags kann man in der Disko tanzen und sich gut amüsieren.
> • Der Fitnessraum ist täglich ab 8 Uhr geöffnet.
> • Unser Schwimmbad ist nur für Kinder ab acht Jahren geöffnet.
>
> Leider haben wir keinen Parkplatz am Hotel, aber Sie können in der Tiefgarage am Martktplatz gratis parken.
>
> *Hotel zum Markt*

Read the following sentences. Write **T** (True), **F** (False) or **?** (Not in the text) in the box.

(a) The hotel is next door to the town hall. ☐ *(1 mark)*

(b) The hotel has modern facilities. ☐ *(1 mark)*

(c) The hotel will have air conditioning soon. ☐ *(1 mark)*

> The statements to identify are in the same order as the text – follow the text through with the statements.

(d) The bedrooms are spacious. ☐ *(1 mark)*

(e) The swimming pool is open to children of all ages. ☐ *(1 mark)*

(f) The restaurant comes highly recommended. ☐ *(1 mark)*

(g) You can watch a film every evening. ☐ *(1 mark)*

(h) Off-site parking is free. ☐ *(1 mark)*

Staying in a hotel

44 Listen to Verena talking about her hotel stay. Complete the sentences.

(a) Verena stayed at the hotel for .... *(1 mark)*

(b) The hotel often gets booked up .... *(1 mark)*

(c) Verena and her boyfriend wanted a room with .... *(1 mark)*

(d) They ended up in .... *(1 mark)*

(e) The best thing about the room was .... *(1 mark)*

> Make sure you write your answers clearly – don't lose marks by being careless because your answer is not easy to read.

Staying on a campsite

Camping at the seaside

45 Marina has been sent a leaflet about a campsite.

What does the campsite offer?

A	Closeness to the beach
B	Camping all year
C	Cheap camping
D	A restaurant
E	A swimming pool
F	A shop
G	Boat hire
H	Dancing
I	Cycle hire

Zelten am Meer!

- Tolles Zelten nicht weit vom Strand – nur fünf Minuten zu Fuß.
- Wir haben nur im Winter geschlossen (November bis März).
- Zelten ist sehr billig: 12,50 € pro Nacht.
- Vor Ort finden Sie einen Laden und einen Schnellimbiss.
- Man kann viel machen:
  - im Meer schwimmen
  - am Samstagabend bis 23:00 Uhr tanzen gehen
  - in den Aufenthaltsraum gehen. (Sehr gut, wenn es regnet!)
  - Fahrräder ausleihen und sich die schöne Gegend ansehen.
- Am Samstagvormittag gibt es in der Nachbarstadt einen großen Markt.

Guten Aufenthalt!

Write the **four** correct letters in the boxes.

Example: A ☐ ☐ ☐ ☐

(4 marks)

My camping holidays

46 Listen to Bianca talking about her camping experience. Write the correct letter in the box.

(a) Camping is enjoyed by …

A	Bianca's mother
B	Bianca
C	Bianca's father

☐ *(1 mark)*

(b) Bianca enjoys …

A	reading
B	annoying her brother
C	playing computer games

☐ *(1 mark)*

(c) Bianca also enjoys …

A	chatting with other teenagers
B	walking in the wood
C	the food at the café

☐ *(1 mark)*

(d) Bianca thinks …

A	food tastes better at home than at a barbecue
B	barbecue food tastes better than food at home
C	the disco is fun

☐ *(1 mark)*

41

Had a go ☐   Nearly there ☐   Nailed it! ☐

Holiday activities

A

READING

Holiday forum

47 You read part of an online discussion about holiday activities.

○ ○ ○

◄ ► ⟳ ✄ +   Q▾

Hannah (18) aus Hamburg schreibt:

Wir freuen uns alle auf den Sommerurlaub, weil wir uns alle am Ende des langen Schuljahres ein paar Wochen lang gut amüsieren und ausruhen wollen.

Meine Freunde fahren lieber ohne Eltern weg. Sie reisen zum Beispiel mit der Bahn ins Ausland, weil sie das wärmere Klima lieben. Sie bleiben meistens an der Küste, wo es viel für junge Leute zu tun gibt. Zum Beispiel können sie den ganzen Tag schwimmen, am Strand liegen und mit den Freunden Volleyball oder Fußball spielen.

Abends ist immer viel los. Man tanzt bis spät in die Nacht oder man unterhält sich in Cafés und Lokalen. Weil diese Urlauber ohne Eltern reisen und so spät ins Bett gehen, stehen sie vormittags gewöhnlich nicht sehr früh auf.

Normalerweise machen sie auch gern Ausflüge zu historischen Sehenswürdigkeiten wie Burgen und alten Kirchen, weil sie gern Fotos von ihnen machen und sie oft im Bus ein bisschen schlafen können. Sie unterhalten sich aber am liebsten am Strand. Dieses Jahr wird sich das aber ändern. Die Polizei wird an solchen Urlaubsorten strenger werden. Diesen Sommer wird es verboten sein, Alkohol am Strand zu trinken und ohne T-Shirts und Schuhe Kneipen zu besuchen. Mal sehen, ob sich die jungen Besucher aus aller Welt besser benehmen werden.

(a) Why exactly does Hannah think young people look forward to the summer holiday?

.... *(1 mark)*

(b) What is the attraction of a foreign holiday?

.... *(1 mark)*

(c) Why can the holiday-makers go to bed late?

.... *(1 mark)*

(d) Why do young people enjoy visiting historic sites?

.... *(1 mark)*

(e) What is going to change this year at some resorts?

.... *(1 mark)*

(f) What is Hannah's opinion of the change?

.... *(1 mark)*

C

LISTENING
40

An active holiday

48 Listen to Andreas talking about what he did on holiday.

What did he do?

| A | B | C | D | E | F |

Write the **three** correct letters in the boxes.

(3 marks)

Holiday preferences

Holiday blogs

49 These teenagers have blogged about their holiday preferences.

> **Nils:** Ich mache lieber Urlaub in einem Hotel in der Nähe vom Meer, wo ich den ganzen Tag in der Sonne am Strand liegen kann.
>
> **Bernadette:** Zelten auf dem Land finde ich normalerweise prima, besonders wenn es auf dem Campingplatz ein Schwimmbad gibt. Letztes Jahr hatten wir aber Pech, weil es die ganze Zeit geregnet hat. Das war mies, weil wir draußen weder grillen noch spielen konnten.
>
> **Tom:** Ich ziehe Sporturlaube vor, weil ich sehr aktiv bin. Am liebsten fahre ich in eine Jugendherberge in den Bergen, wo man klettern und wandern kann. Das einzige Problem ist, dass wir nicht klettern gehen dürfen, wenn es zu windig ist, weil das gefährlich sein könnte.
>
> **Lea:** Sieben Nächte auf einem Schiff auf der Donau. Spitze! Es ist immer ganz ruhig auf dem Fluss, aber letztes Mal gab es leider ein großes Gewitter und wir mussten alle eine Nacht im Hotel in der Stadt verbringen. Schade.

A	B	C	D	E	F

1	2	3	4	5	6

What weather and holiday accommodation do these teenagers mention?

Write the correct letters and numbers in the table.

	Weather	Accommodation	
Example: Nils	C	2	
Bernadette			*(2 marks)*
Tom			*(2 marks)*
Lea			*(2 marks)*

Holiday activities

50 Listen to Svenja and Lutz talking about what they enjoy doing on holiday.

A	Sitting on the beach	C	Doing team sports	E	Camping holidays	G	Hiking
B	Snowboarding	D	Active holidays	F	Family holidays	H	Shopping

(a) What does Svenja enjoy doing on holiday?
Write the **two** correct letters in the boxes.

☐ ☐   *(2 marks)*

(b) What does Lutz enjoy doing on holiday?
Write the **two** correct letters in the boxes.

☐ ☐   *(2 marks)*

> Watch out for negatives here – you may hear the activities mentioned, but does the speaker enjoy doing them?

Holiday plans

B

Holiday plans

51 Read Alexander's letter to his grandfather about his holiday plans.

> Lieber Opa,
>
> vielen Dank für das Geld. Es ist sehr nützlich, weil ich einen besseren Rucksack für den Urlaub brauche. Ich werde mit meinem Freund Markus durch Frankreich und Spanien reisen.
>
> Am vierten September fahren wir los. Ich bin schon sehr gespannt! Markus hat ein Motorrad und die Reise wird viel Spaß machen. Wenn das Geld reicht, bleiben wir vier Wochen lang weg.
>
> Obwohl wir meistens zelten werden, wollen wir ab und zu auch in kleinen Hotels schlafen. Dann werden wir abends in einem billigen Restaurant essen, weil wir nicht zu viel Geld ausgeben wollen.
>
> Wir werden in einigen Städten ein bisschen länger bleiben, um die besten Sehenswürdigkeiten zu besuchen. Natürlich wollen wir unterwegs auch ein paar nette Mädchen kennenlernen!
>
> Ich schicke dir viele Postkarten!
>
> Viele Grüße von
>
> Alexander

Read the following statements. Which **four** are correct?

A	Alexander is writing to his grandfather.
B	Alexander has a rucksack from his grandfather.
C	Alexander plans to travel outside Germany.
D	Alexander hopes to be away two months.
E	Alexander will use his friend's transport.
F	Alexander will only stay on campsites.
G	Alexander will vary how long he stays in places.
H	Alexander will do some sightseeing.
I	Alexander will email his grandfather.

Write the **four** correct letters in the boxes.

Example:

[A] [ ] [ ] [ ] [ ]   *(4 marks)*

A

Plans for a holiday

52 Listen to Yannick asking Linda about her holiday plans.

(a) (i) Why is Linda keen to go to America?

.... *(1 mark)*

(ii) Why does she think she can stay with her aunt?

.... *(1 mark)*

(iii) Why does she want to get to know the country now?

.... *(1 mark)*

(b) (i) How does she hope her cousin will help her?

.... *(1 mark)*

(ii) Why exactly is Linda excited about her winter holiday this year?

.... *(1 mark)*

Past holidays

A holiday report

53 Leah has written a report about her holiday.

> Die Reise im letzten August zum Bodensee war ziemlich lang, aber mein Vater hatte alles gut geplant. Unser Auto ist alt und wir haben regelmäßig an Raststätten auf der Autobahn anhalten müssen.
>
> Meine Eltern hatten eine kleine Wohnung mit einer schönen Aussicht auf den See gemietet. Die Unterkunft war besser, als sie erwartet hatten.
>
> Das Wetter war wechselhaft, aber es hat nicht zu viel geregnet. Der Tagesausflug mit der Fähre in die Schweiz war sehr schön, weil es den ganzen Tag sonnig war. Wir haben auch einige interessante Schlösser in der Umgebung besucht. Die kleinen Städte waren hübsch und sehr sauber, aber die Straßen waren steil und sehr eng. Es gab viele Touristen und es war schwer zu laufen.
>
> Es war ein toller Sommerurlaub. Nächstes Jahr will ich unbedingt noch einmal dorthin zurückfahren, obwohl meine Familie nach Spanien fährt. Ich würde lieber mit Freunden Urlaub am Bodensee machen und will nicht ins Ausland reisen.

> If you change your mind about an answer, cross it out and write the corrected one in the box clearly.

Write the correct letter in the box.

(a) What sort of holiday is Leah describing?

A	A holiday with friends
B	A winter holiday
C	A family holiday

☐   *(1 mark)*

(b) When did the holiday take place?

A	In April
B	Two years ago
C	Last year

☐   *(1 mark)*

(c) What did Leah's father do?

A	Hired a car
B	Organised the trip
C	Drove too fast

☐   *(1 mark)*

(d) How does Leah rate the accommodation?

A	Exceeded expectations
B	Disappointing
C	Average

☐   *(1 mark)*

(e) What sort of weather did they have?

A	Dreadful
B	Always raining
C	Sometimes good

☐   *(1 mark)*

(f) What modes of transport did Leah use on the holiday?

A	Car and ship
B	Car
C	Ship and bicycle

☐   *(1 mark)*

(g) What did Leah think of the day trip?

A	It was entirely positive
B	It had some drawbacks
C	It was a complete disappointment

☐   *(1 mark)*

(h) What would Leah like to do next year?

A	Go abroad
B	Return to Bodensee with friends
C	Go on holiday with her family

☐   *(1 mark)*

Countries

Countries and nationalities

1   Read these people's online profiles.

> **Jusuf:**
>
> Ich bin in Schottland geboren, aber jetzt wohne ich in Hamburg, Deutschland.

> **Susi:**
>
> Ich heiße Susi und bin sechzehn Jahre alt. Mein Vater kommt aus Irland.

> **Elias:**
> Ich heiße Elias, aber meine Freunde sagen Eli. Meine Mutter ist Engländerin, aber mein Vater kommt aus der Türkei.

> **Leila:**
>
> Ich wohne in Berlin, aber ich habe sechs Jahre in den Vereinigten Staaten gewohnt.

> **Maria:**
> Ich wohne mit meiner Mutter in einer schönen Wohnung in Paris. Meine Mutter ist Französin.

> **Adam:**
> Ich bin am vierten Oktober 1999 in der Schweiz geboren, aber jetzt wohne ich in Österreich.

Write the initial of the person: **J** (Jusuf), **E** (Elias), etc.

Who …

(a) lived in America?   ☐   *(1 mark)*

(b) is half Irish?   ☐   *(1 mark)*

(c) was born in Switzerland?   ☐   *(1 mark)*

(d) has a French parent?   ☐   *(1 mark)*

Backgrounds

2   Listen to Hannes, Sandra and Freddy talking about their backgrounds.

Choose the statement which applies to each speaker.

> **A** 'I would like to live in the country where I was born.'
>
> **B** 'My mum is Swiss and my dad is German.'
>
> **C** 'I speak English and German at home.'
>
> **D** 'When I was a child I lived in Germany.'
>
> **E** 'I live in Switzerland.'

Write the correct letter in the box.

(a) Hannes   ☐   *(1 mark)*

(b) Sandra   ☐   *(1 mark)*

(c) Freddy   ☐   *(1 mark)*

> Watch out for distractors in the passage – you have to hear precise details of what is in the statements A–E above to be able to allocate each one to a person.

My house

Flat advert

3 Read the newspaper advert for a flat.

> ## Freundliche helle 4-Zimmer-Wohnung im Schwarzwald
>
> Diese ruhige Mietwohnung liegt im Schwarzwald und ist 120 m² groß. Sie befindet sich im Erdgeschoss eines modernen, sehr beliebten Wohnblocks.
>
> Die Wohnung hat zwei große Schlafzimmer, ein geräumiges Wohnzimmer und eine moderne Küche mit Essecke. Es gibt auch ein Gäste-WC und einen Keller mit Waschmaschine.
>
> Im Badezimmer erwartet Sie eine wunderbare Überraschung – eine Luxusdusche mit Radio und Massagekopf.
>
> Die Wohnung liegt in einer ruhigen Gegend am Rande von Freiburg. Nebenan befindet sich ein Supermarkt, in dem man schnell und einfach einkaufen kann.
>
> Öffentliche Einrichtungen wie Bank, Arztpraxis, Apotheke sowie Kindergärten und Schulen sind alle am Ort zu finden.
>
> Es gibt gute Anbindungen an öffentliche Verkehrsmittel und ein autofreies Leben wäre hier möglich.
>
> Sportliche Menschen finden hier ein reiches Angebot an Freizeitmöglichkeiten, wie Freibad, Sporthalle und Sportplatz.
>
> **Extras:**
> * Wintergarten, Balkon, große Terrasse und Garage
> * Familien mit Kindern willkommen
> * Haustiere sind erlaubt
> * Einzug ab September möglich

Which **four** statements are correct?

A   This flat is for sale.

B   You don't need a car to live here.

C   There is a spacious dining room.

D   You can't walk to the shops.

E   The bathroom contains a special feature.

F   The local amenities are good.

G   The public transport is poor.

H   There is a selection of sports facilities nearby.

Write the **four** correct letters in the boxes. ☐ ☐ ☐ ☐   *(4 marks)*

A house viewing

4 Listen to Frau Gottschalk talking about a house she viewed yesterday.

What did she think of the house?

Write **P** for positive. Write **N** for negative.

Write **P + N** for positive and negative.

(a) ☐   *(1 mark)*

> Listen to the entire extract before you answer each one – a positive opinion might also contain a negative element.

(b) ☐   *(1 mark)*

(c) ☐   *(1 mark)*

(d) ☐   *(1 mark)*

Had a go ☐   Nearly there ☐   Nailed it! ☐

My room

Peter's room

5 Read Peter's email about his room.

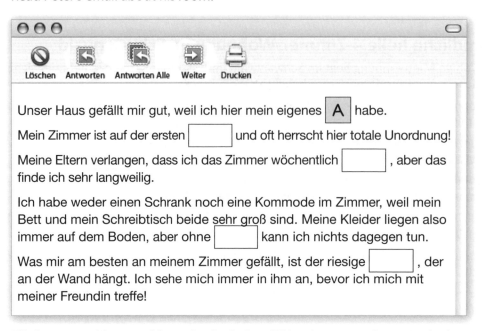

Löschen   Antworten   Antworten Alle   Weiter   Drucken

Unser Haus gefällt mir gut, weil ich hier mein eigenes **A** habe.

Mein Zimmer ist auf der ersten ☐ und oft herrscht hier totale Unordnung!

Meine Eltern verlangen, dass ich das Zimmer wöchentlich ☐ , aber das finde ich sehr langweilig.

Ich habe weder einen Schrank noch eine Kommode im Zimmer, weil mein Bett und mein Schreibtisch beide <u>sehr groß</u> sind. Meine Kleider liegen also immer auf dem Boden, aber ohne ☐ kann ich nichts dagegen tun.

Was mir am besten an meinem Zimmer gefällt, ist der riesige ☐ , der an der Wand hängt. Ich sehe mich immer in ihm an, bevor ich mich mit meiner Freundin treffe!

Fill the gaps with a word from the list below. Write the correct letter in the box.

A	Zimmer
B	Decken
C	aufräume

D	Etage
E	Spiegel
F	Vorhang

G	Möbel
H	Erdgeschoss
I	verlasse

(4 marks)

Room items

6 Listen to people talking about items for their room. Write the correct letter in the box.

(a) What is Michael's favourite item?

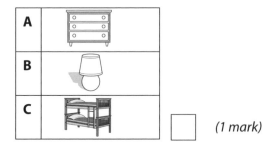

☐ *(1 mark)*

(c) What does Felix need for his room?

☐ *(1 mark)*

(b) What is Gabi looking for?

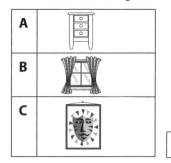

☐ *(1 mark)*

(d) What is Stefanie looking for?

☐ *(1 mark)*

Helping at home

Chores

7   Read Konrad's blog about how he helps at home.

> Ich wohne mit meinen Eltern und meiner kleinen Schwester im Westen von Deutschland.
>
> Meine Eltern gehen beide zur Arbeit und ich muss viel im Haushalt helfen. Das finde ich fair, aber manchmal geht es mir auf die Nerven.
>
> Einkaufen zum Beispiel: Der Supermarkt liegt zehn Minuten mit dem Rad entfernt und ich finde es so mühsam, dorthin zu fahren, die Lebensmittel abzuholen, dafür zu zahlen und dann wieder nach Hause zu fahren. Ich würde viel lieber das Auto waschen, weil das zumindest Spaß macht, besonders wenn es sonnig ist.
>
> Im Sommer muss ich auch ab und zu den Rasen mähen, aber ich finde das anstrengend und mein Vater wird immer böse, wenn ich das nicht perfekt erledige.
>
> Wenn meine Eltern spät von der Arbeit zurückkommen oder abends ausgehen, passe ich gern auf meine kleine Schwester auf. Das finde ich toll, weil wir gut miteinander auskommen und das Babysitten kein Problem ist. Ich bin aber froh, dass wir keine Haustiere haben, sonst würde ich sie sicher täglich füttern müssen!

> Underline key words related to the pictures below – then look for the opinion which goes with each one.

| A | B | C | D | E | F |

(a) Which **two** chores does Konrad enjoy doing? Write the **two** correct letters in the boxes.

☐ ☐   *(2 marks)*

(b) Which **two** chores does he not enjoy doing? Write the **two** correct letters in the boxes.

☐ ☐   *(2 marks)*

> Read the question carefully – don't ignore important words like 'not'.

Can't go out

8   Listen to Iris and Thomas being invited to go out.

(a) (i) Why exactly can't Iris go to the cinema?

....   *(1 mark)*

(ii) Why does she need to stay at home?

....   *(1 mark)*

(b) (i) Why can't Thomas go ice skating?

....   *(1 mark)*

(ii) What does he feel about this?

....   *(1 mark)*

Where I live

My home

9 Ali has sent his penfriend an email.

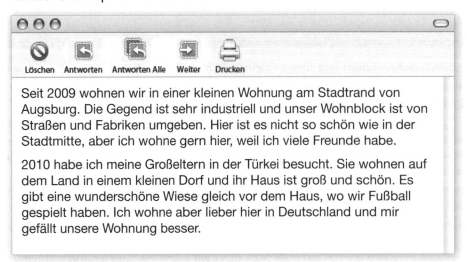

Löschen Antworten Antworten Alle Weiter Drucken

Seit 2009 wohnen wir in einer kleinen Wohnung am Stadtrand von Augsburg. Die Gegend ist sehr industriell und unser Wohnblock ist von Straßen und Fabriken umgeben. Hier ist es nicht so schön wie in der Stadtmitte, aber ich wohne gern hier, weil ich viele Freunde habe.

2010 habe ich meine Großeltern in der Türkei besucht. Sie wohnen auf dem Land in einem kleinen Dorf und ihr Haus ist groß und schön. Es gibt eine wunderschöne Wiese gleich vor dem Haus, wo wir Fußball gespielt haben. Ich wohne aber lieber hier in Deutschland und mir gefällt unsere Wohnung besser.

Which **four** statements are correct?

A Ali lives on the outskirts of a town.

B There are no factories in Ali's area.

C Ali's friends all live in the centre of town.

D His area is not as nice as in the town centre.

E Ali's grandparents live in a flat.

F Ali's grandparents live in a village.

G Ali prefers his home to that of his grandparents.

H Ali played football at a park.

Write the **four** correct letters in the boxes.

☐ ☐ ☐ ☐

(4 marks)

> Read the statements very carefully and look for details in the text.

A new home

10 Listen to Silke talking about her new home.

(a) Give a positive and negative aspect of life in Berlin.

(i) Positive:

.... *(1 mark)*

(ii) Negative:

.... *(1 mark)*

(b) Give a positive and negative aspect of where Silke lives now.

(i) Positive:

.... *(1 mark)*

(ii) Negative:

.... *(1 mark)*

Places in town

Going into town

11 Where are these people going?

Doris   Ich gehe ins Kino.

Marta   Ich gehe zum Rathaus.

Markus   Ich gehe zum Spielplatz.

Paul   Ich gehe zum Bahnhof.

Viktoria   Ich gehe in die Bibliothek.

Stefanie   Ich gehe ins Einkaufszentrum.

Johann   Ich gehe in die Kirche.

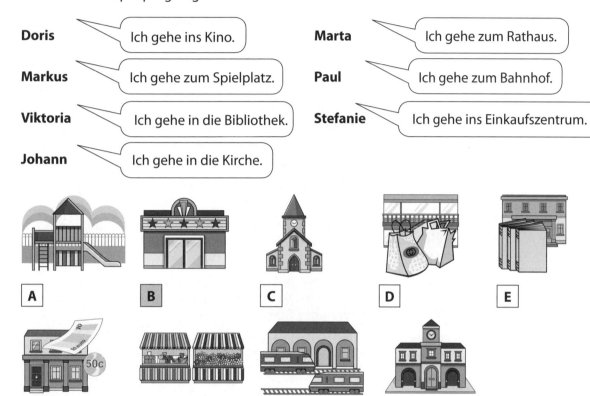

Complete the table by writing the correct letter.

Example: Doris	B
Markus	
Viktoria	
Johann	
Marta	
Paul	
Stefanie	

(1 mark)
(1 mark)
(1 mark)
(1 mark)
(1 mark)
(1 mark)

Places near me

12 Listen to people talking about the place they live near to.

Example: What does Thomas live near to? .... *cathedral* ....

What does ...

(a) Sabine live near to?   ....   *(1 mark)*

(b) Hannes live near to?   ....   *(1 mark)*

(c) Joachim live near to?   ....   *(1 mark)*

(d) Mia live near to?   ....   *(1 mark)*

What to do in town

Visiting Bremen

13 Read the magazine article about Bremen.

Bremen

Jedes Jahr kommen viele Touristen nach Bremen und sie kommen oft noch einmal zurück. Warum? Weil diese norddeutsche Stadt so viel bietet: Geschichte, tolle Einkaufsmöglichkeiten, ein gutes Nachtleben, schöne Spaziergänge.

Sie finden hier preiswerte Unterkunft, aber während des Weihnachtsmarktes sollten Sie im Voraus buchen, weil Hotels und auch Jugendherbergen schnell ausgebucht sind.

Mit der „Erlebniscard Bremen" kann man billiger mit öffentlichen Verkehrsmitteln fahren. Außerdem bekommt man mit dieser Karte Ermäßigungen für Theater, Führungen usw.

Im Schnoorviertel finden Sie allerlei interessante Geschäfte, wo Sie Andenken oder Geschenke kaufen können. Danach sollten Sie in den Kneipen und Restaurants die Spezialitäten der Stadt genießen.

Jeder Besucher wird in den vielen verschiedenen Museen etwas Interessantes finden. Vergessen Sie aber nicht, dass die meisten Museen montags geschlossen sind.

> Make sure you have revised 'little' words such as *jeder* (each) and *dieser* (this). The more words you easily recognise, the easier the task will be.

(a) How do you know that many tourists like coming to Bremen?

.... *(1 mark)*

(b) What should tourists be aware of at Christmas time?

Write the correct letter in the box. ☐

    A   They should book accommodation early

    B   Youth hostels are not recommended

    C   All accommodation will cost more   *(1 mark)*

(c) What advice is given about public transport?

.... *(1 mark)*

(d) What exactly has Schnoorviertel got to offer shoppers?

.... *(1 mark)*

(e) What do the tourists need to know if they are planning to visit a museum?

.... *(1 mark)*

Tourist attractions

At the tourist office

14 You read this notice in the visitor centre.

Herzlich willkommen!

In unserer Stadt gibt es viel zu tun.

Man kann von Dienstag bis Sonntag, 10:30–16:30 Uhr, das interessante Stadtmuseum besuchen. Nach dem Besuch kann man im Café im Erdgeschoss essen und trinken oder im Museumsgeschäft einkaufen gehen.

Nächsten Sonntag kann man einen Ausflug in die wunderbare Stadt Bonn machen. Wir fahren um 8:30 Uhr vom Busbahnhof ab. Man kann viele Sehenswürdigkeiten vom Bus aus sehen und auch Fotos machen.

Die tolle Kunstgalerie im Rathaus ist von 10:00 bis 17:00 Uhr geöffnet. Sie ist montags geschlossen.

Am Donnerstag gibt es einen Rundgang durch die Stadt. Er beginnt um 11:00 Uhr am Dom und ist perfekt für Kinder. Am Ende geht man den Fluss entlang und verbringt eine Stunde im Park.

A	art gallery	**D**	town hall	**G**	bus station
B	cathedral	**E**	Tuesday–Sunday		
C	river	**F**	tour of the town		

Write the correct letter in the box to complete the sentences.

Example: The museum is open **E** .

(a) The ☐ is closed on Mondays.   *(1 mark)*

(b) The Bonn trip leaves from the ☐. *(1 mark)*

(c) The art gallery is in the ☐. *(1 mark)*

(d) Children will enjoy the ☐. *(1 mark)*

Local information

15 Listen to Vitali asking for information about the local area. Write the correct letter in the box.

(a) The tourist office recommends a …

A	walk round the town
B	city tour
C	tour of the cathedral

☐ *(1 mark)*

(b) The tourist office recommends …

A	taking photos of the church
B	going to a church service
C	climbing the church tower

☐ *(1 mark)*

(c) You can catch a bus to the swimming pool from the …

A	bus station
B	town hall
C	market place

☐ *(1 mark)*

(d) In the evenings you can …

A	go dancing
B	go to a pub
C	go for a walk

☐ *(1 mark)*

> Use a process of elimination to help you identify the answer – cross out any options you know to be wrong after a first listening.

Signs in town

F **Notices**

16 You see these signs in town.

A Der Schnellimbiss ist jeden Tag geöffnet.

B Kinder sind im Museum immer willkommen.

C Radfahren in der Fußgängerzone ist verboten.

D Die Toiletten sind neben dem Eingang.

E Tür bitte drücken.

F Am Bahnhof darf man nicht rauchen.

G Abfall bitte hineinwerfen.

Write the correct letter in the box.

Which sign tells you …

Example: where the toilets are?   D

(a) not to cycle?   ☐   *(1 mark)*

(b) to push the door?   ☐   *(1 mark)*

(c) not to smoke?   ☐   *(1 mark)*

(d) where to throw your rubbish?   ☐   *(1 mark)*

C **Jutta's trip to town**

17 Listen to Jutta talking about her trip to town.

(a) How does Jutta feel after her trip to town?

....   *(1 mark)*

(b) Why exactly did Jutta go to the shopping centre?

....   *(1 mark)*

(c) How did Jutta feel after her visit to the shopping centre?

....   *(1 mark)*

(d) What could she *not* find? Write the correct letter in the box.

> Read the question carefully – here you need the place or item Jutta did **not** find.

A   **B**   **C**   ☐   *(1 mark)*

54

Pros and cons of your town

Opinions about a town

18 Read what these people say about their town.

Felix:	Meine Stadt hat viel anzubieten. Für Kinder ist sie besonders gut, weil es ein neues Freizeitzentrum, zwei ☐ , ein Theater usw. gibt. Leider gibt es aber auch viel Verkehr und das finde ich sehr ☐ .
Lilli:	Ich wohne in einer kleinen Stadt. Es gibt hier nichts zu tun, weil wir kein Kino und kein Sportzentrum haben. Wir fahren oft in die nächste Stadt, weil dort die ☐ gut sind und wir gern einkaufen gehen.
Sophie:	Ich liebe meine Stadt, aber sie hat einen großen ☐ : im Sommer kommen zu viele Touristen hierher, weil die Stadt so hübsch ist. Dann sind die Cafés am Marktplatz immer voll und das finde ich nicht so gut.

Fill in the gaps in the text with words from the table. Write the correct letter in the box.

A	Nachteil		**C**	Vorteil		**E**	Städte		**G**	Geschäfte
B	laut		**D**	Kneipe		**F**	ruhig		**H**	Kinos

(4 marks)

Two opinions on Freiburg

19 Listen to Milos and Leonie giving their opinion about Freiburg.

Milos

(a) Where exactly is Freiburg?

.... *(1 mark)*

(b) Why is it not a problem if you live outside of the town?

.... *(1 mark)*

(c) Name **two** other advantages Milos mentions about Freiburg.

(i) .... *(1 mark)*

(ii) .... *(1 mark)*

(d) What does Milos's family do when they go on holiday?

.... *(1 mark)*

Leonie

(a) What is Leonie's main complaint about Freiburg?

.... *(1 mark)*

(b) Why exactly does she find things worse in the summer?

.... *(1 mark)*

(c) Where would she prefer to live?

.... *(1 mark)*

(d) Why is that not possible?

.... *(1 mark)*

Town description

Ivan's town

20 Read Ivan's blog about his town.

> Wir sind endlich umgezogen und ich wohne gern hier, obwohl mir meine Freunde in Gütersloh fehlen. Glücklicherweise bleiben wir mit Hilfe des Computers in Kontakt, weil ich mich hier in Nordostdeutschland wie im Ausland fühle! Die Stadt ist interessant und hat fast doppelt so viele Einwohner wie Gütersloh. Wir wohnen in einer ruhigen Umgebung, wo die Luft viel frischer als in der Innenstadt ist. Dort kann die Luftverschmutzung im Sommer unerträglich werden, habe ich gehört.
>
> Ich finde es toll, dass es hier wegen der Studentenbevölkerung so viele Sportklubs, Stadien und Schwimmbäder gibt. Wir wohnen nicht weit von einem neuen Freizeitzentrum entfernt und ich bin dort schon Mitglied des Handballklubs.
>
> Die Stadt hat zwei sehr große Universitäten und das ist prima, weil die Geschäfte und Cafés besonders gut für junge Leute sind. Sie sind oft ziemlich preiswert und haben Angebote für Studenten. Ein Nachteil davon ist aber, dass es samstagnachts immer Krach im Stadtzentrum gibt – ich war letztes Wochenende dabei, aber das werde ich nie wieder machen!

(a) What does Ivan compare his new home area to?

.... *(1 mark)*

(b) What **two** things does Ivan say about the air quality?

(i) .... *(1 mark)*

(ii) .... *(1 mark)*

(c) What is a positive and negative aspect of living in a student town?

(i) Positive:

.... *(1 mark)*

(ii) Negative:

.... *(1 mark)*

> Die Stadt ist nicht sehr modern, aber das Einkaufszentrum ist toll und es gibt mehrere Kinos und Nachtklubs. Jeden Samstag gibt es im Schlossgarten ein Konzert und letztes Wochenende bin ich dahin gegangen, weil meine Lieblingsgruppe auf dem Programm stand. Die neue Eishalle neben dem Bahnhof ist bei Jugendlichen besonders beliebt, aber ich bin noch nie dahin gegangen.
>
> Viele Einwohner arbeiten in den verschiedenen Fabriken am Stadtrand, wo man zum Beispiel Autos und Flugzeuge baut. Zur Hauptverkehrszeit fahren viele Autos und Lastwagen und gibt es deshalb lange Staus.

(d) What activity has Ivan joined in with in his new town?

.... *(1 mark)*

(e) What does Ivan say about the traffic situation in the town?

.... *(1 mark)*

> Keep your answers close to the content of the text.
> Don't make assumptions.

Weather

The forecast

21 Read the weather forecast for Austria.

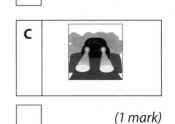

Austria

A Am Vormittag donnert und blitzt es.	**E** Im Osten ist es wolkig.
B Es regnet in Wien.	**F** In der Nacht gibt es im Westen Nebel.
C Im Süden scheint den ganzen Tag die Sonne.	**G** Morgen schneit es.
D Am Nachmittag ist es ziemlich kalt.	

Write the correct letter in the box.

Which item mentions …

(a) rain? ☐   *(1 mark)*   **(d)** fog? ☐   *(1 mark)*

(b) the temperature? ☐   *(1 mark)*   **(e)** sunshine? ☐   *(1 mark)*

(c) a thunderstorm? ☐   *(1 mark)*

Weather reports

22 Listen to the radio weather reports. What is the weather forecast for these towns? Write the correct letter in the box.

(a) Kiel:

      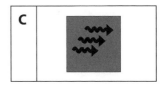

☐ *(1 mark)*

(b) Rosenheim:

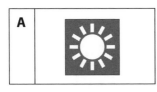      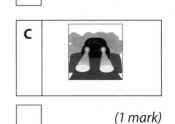

☐ *(1 mark)*

(c) Ludwigsburg:

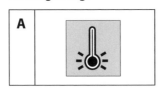   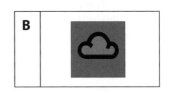   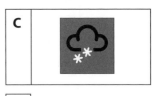

☐ *(1 mark)*

Listen carefully for any negatives, for example, *kein / keinen.*

Celebrations at home

A   An invitation

23 You receive details about a wedding.

(a) In what order are these items mentioned in the invitation? Write 1 against the first item, 2 against the second and 3 against the third.

Gift	☐
What will happen after the ceremony	☐
Accommodation	☐

(1 mark)

> Liebe Freundinnen und Freunde,
>
> Ihr habt die Einladung zur Hochzeit ja schon per E-Mail bekommen. Wir möchten euch zu unserer Hochzeitsfeier einladen. Die Trauung findet am Samstag den 3. Oktober um 14:00 Uhr statt. Danach laden wir euch alle zu uns nach Hause ein, wo wir zusammen essen und trinken werden. Nach dem Abendessen wird der Abend gemütlich mit Musikunterhaltung weitergehen. Um Mitternacht wird unser höchst großzügige Nachbarn ein Feuerwerk im Garten nebenan geben.
>
> Bitte meldet euch rechtzeitig, wenn ihr einen Übernachtungsplatz benötigt. Wir können euch Gästebetten im Hotel nebenan reservieren.
>
> Als Geschenk bitten wir um Geld.
>
> Wir freuen uns so auf diesen einmaligen Tag, an dem wir zusammen feiern können.
>
> Kinder und Hunde willkommen!

(b) What is the letter inviting people to?

.... *(1 mark)*

(c) Mention **two** things which Ulli and Herbert are organising for their guests.

(i) .... *(1 mark)*

(ii) .... *(1 mark)*

(d) What do Ulli and Herbert think of their neighbours?

.... *(1 mark)*

> Break up long words such as *Hochzeitsfeier – Hochzeit* (wedding) + *Feier* (party), to help your understanding – you may well know the smaller words which make up the long word.

D   Christmas

24 Listen to Lily and Emil talking about Christmas. What do they find good about it?

A	The parties	**C**	The company
B	The presents	**D**	The food

Write the correct letter in the box.

(a) Lily ☐   *(1 mark)*

(b) Emil ☐   *(1 mark)*

Directions

How do I get there?

25 Read the directions sent to you by text message.

Du stehst am Rathaus, nicht? Geh also geradeaus bis zur Bibliothek, dann geh über die Kreuzung und nimm die dritte Straße links. Nimm die nächste Straße rechts und geh dann geradeaus. An der Ampel geh nach rechts. Geh dann 50 Meter weiter, am Krankenhaus vorbei. Der Park ist auf der rechten Seite neben der Sporthalle.

Complete the instructions.

Example: You are at the .....town hall.....................

(a) You go straight ahead until you come to the ....   *(1 mark)*

(b) After the .... you take the third road on the left.   *(1 mark)*

(c) At the traffic lights you turn ....   *(1 mark)*

(d) The park is on the right-hand side after the ....   *(1 mark)*

> Always check through your answers at the end of the exam to avoid careless mistakes.

Directions in town

26 Listen to the directions. What are these people being told to do?

A	Cross the bridge
B	Go round the corner
C	Turn left at the lights
D	Go left at the crossroads
E	Go right at the roundabout
F	Carry straight on
G	Turn right at the lights

Write the correct letter in the box.

Example: A

(a) ☐   *(1 mark)*   (c) ☐   *(1 mark)*

(b) ☐   *(1 mark)*   (d) ☐   *(1 mark)*

At the train station

Station signs

27 Read these signs at the station.

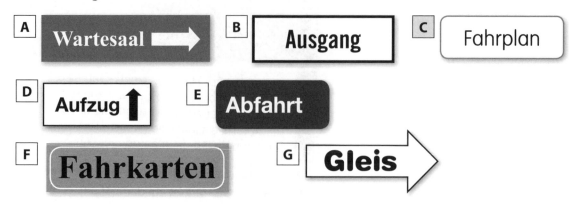

A Wartesaal ➡	B Ausgang	C Fahrplan
D Aufzug ⬆	E Abfahrt	
F Fahrkarten	G Gleis ➡	

Which sign do these people need to follow? Write the correct letter in the box.

Example: Where are the timetables? | C |

(a) Is there somewhere warm I can wait? ☐ *(1 mark)*

(b) How do I get out of here? ☐ *(1 mark)*

(c) I'm looking for platform 10b. ☐ *(1 mark)*

(d) Where can I buy a ticket? ☐ *(1 mark)*

> Match the signs you are confident of first, then go back and try to work out the others.

Station information

28 Listen to the passengers asking for information at the station. What are they looking for?

A Lift	B Departures	C Left luggage
D Waiting room	E Ticket office	

Listen and write the correct letter in the box.

(a) ☐ *(1 mark)*

(b) ☐ *(1 mark)*

(c) ☐ *(1 mark)*

Travelling

Means of transport

29 Read how these people travel.

Iris   Ich fahre gern mit dem Boot auf dem Bodensee.

Beate   Ich fahre mit dem Bus in die Stadt.

Alex   Mein Bruder fährt jeden Tag mit dem Mofa.

Demitri   Ich fliege mit dem Flugzeug nach Berlin.

Gabi   Paul fährt mit dem Auto zum Stadion.

Franz   In London fährt man mit der U-Bahn.

Write the initial of the person: **I** (Iris), **B** (Beate), etc.

(a) Who travels by plane? ☐   *(1 mark)*

(b) Whose brother has a moped? ☐   *(1 mark)*

(c) Who mentions the underground? ☐   *(1 mark)*

(d) Who likes travelling by boat? ☐   *(1 mark)*

How Mustafa travels

30 Listen to Mustafa talking about the ways he travels.

(a) Why does Mustafa **not** go to the sports centre by car?

.... *(1 mark)*

(b) Why does Mustafa go to school by suburban train?

.... *(1 mark)*

Write the correct letter.

(c) What reason does Mustafa give for using the underground?

   A It is free

   B He gets a reduced fare

   C The station is near his house   ☐   *(1 mark)*

(d) What reason does Mustafa give for going by train to Baden-Baden?

   A It is environmentally friendly

   B You can never park there

   C Petrol and parking are expensive   ☐   *(1 mark)*

Transport

Transport

31 Read about Pia's experiences with transport.

> Man sollte am besten mit den öffentlichen Verkehrsmitteln fahren, weil das umweltfreundlich ist. Auf dem Land, wo ich früher gewohnt habe, war das nicht immer möglich und oft ist nur ein Bus pro Tag in die Stadtmitte gefahren und eine Rückfahrkarte hat sehr viel gekostet.
>
> Weil es in der Stadtmitte oft Staus gibt, fahren viele Leute lieber mit der Straßenbahn. Die Straßenbahnen sind pünktlich und die Fahrkarte ist sehr preiswert.
>
> Ich fand die U-Bahn in Berlin toll. Man kann so schnell in der Stadt herumfahren und das ist super praktisch. Mir hat weniger gefallen, dass die Wagen so voll waren. Das kann einem schnell auf die Nerven gehen.
>
> Meine Familie hat kein Auto, aber das ist kein Problem, weil ich nicht gern mit dem Auto fahre – es gibt immer zu viel Verkehr, und die Verschmutzung auf der Autobahn ist schrecklich.
>
> Am allerliebsten fahre ich aber mit dem Rad, weil das gesund, umweltfreundlich und praktisch ist. Man braucht nur ein Rad und einen Helm, und hier gibt es viele Fahrradwege, wo man sicher und sorglos fahren kann.

What does Pia think about these items?

Write **P** for positive.

Write **N** for negative.

Write **P + N** for positive and negative.

> You are looking for opinions here – find the key word and then look for the opinion about it.

(a) Public transport ☐   *(1 mark)*   **(d)** Cars ☐   *(1 mark)*

(b) Trams ☐   *(1 mark)*   **(e)** Bikes ☐   *(1 mark)*

(c) Underground ☐   *(1 mark)*

Kim's opinion

32 Listen to Kim giving her opinion on public transport.

(a) What annoys Kim the most about going on public transport?

.... *(1 mark)*

(b) Why does Kim prefer the car to public transport? Mention **two** reasons.

(i) .... *(1 mark)*

(ii) .... *(1 mark)*

(c) What advantage and disadvantage does Kim give about flying?

(i) Advantage:

.... *(1 mark)*

(ii) Disadvantage:

.... *(1 mark)*

(d) What does Kim think is the best thing about having a bicycle?

.... *(1 mark)*

The environment

Environmental issues

33 Read Petra's letter to a government minister.

> Sehr geehrte Frau Volk,
>
> ich schreibe Ihnen heute, weil ich mir große Sorgen über die Umweltprobleme in unserer Gegend mache.
>
> Es stört mich, dass so viele Leute in unserer Stadt noch überall mit dem Auto hinfahren und ich halte es für ungerecht, dass es erlaubt ist, eine neue Autobahn am Stadtrand zu bauen. Wäre es nicht besser, weniger Straßen zu bauen und bessere öffentliche Verkehrsmittel anzubieten?
>
> Wenn man diese Autobahn baut, wird die Luftverschmutzung in unserer schönen Stadt genauso schlimm wie auf den Straßen von Mexico City oder Bangkok werden und viele Leute werden an den Lärmproblemen leiden.
>
> Ich bitte Sie, dieses Straßenbauprojekt nicht zu unterstützen, damit man die Tiere und Pflanzen in der Umgebung schützen kann. Man würde dabei auch die Luftqualität in der Innenstadt und um die Stadt herum schonen.

(a) What decision has prompted Petra to write this letter?

.... *(1 mark)*

(b) What does Petra suggest as an alternative to road building?

.... *(1 mark)*

(c) What will be the result if the road is built? Mention **two** things.

(i) .... *(1 mark)*

(ii) .... *(1 mark)*

(d) What does Petra hope will be the outcome of her letter? Mention **two** things.

(i) .... *(1 mark)*

(ii) .... *(1 mark)*

Environmental concerns

34 Listen to Sabine and Michael talking about their concerns. Complete the grid.

	Main concern	**Why**	**Solution**	
(a) Sabine				*(3 marks)*
(b) Michael				*(3 marks)*

> For higher listening questions you might have to infer meaning – the answer will not be obvious, but if you understand the extract you should be able to get the correct answer.

Had a go ☐　Nearly there ☐　Nailed it! ☐

Environmental issues

How environmentally friendly are you?

35 Read the survey about the environment.

> ### Bist du umweltfreundlich?
> ### Machst du Folgendes?
> ### Ja oder nein?
>
> 1　Ich trenne den Müll.
>
> 2　Ich fahre mit den öffentlichen Verkehrsmitteln.
>
> 3　Ich fahre mit dem Rad zur Schule.
>
> 4　Ich mache wenig Lärm.
>
> 5　Ich recycle alle Verpackungen.
>
> 6　Ich helfe bedrohten Tieren.

> Don't worry if you don't understand every word in the survey – it might turn out that you don't need to use that sentence for the answers.

Which number could you tick on the survey if you …

(a) don't make noise? ☐ *(1 mark)*　**(c)** help threatened animals? ☐ *(1 mark)*

(b) sort your rubbish? ☐ *(1 mark)*　**(d)** use public transport ☐ *(1 mark)*

Helping the environment

36 Listen to a radio interview about environmental protection.

A　　B　　C　　D　　E　　F

What should people do to help the environment? Write the correct letter.

(a) ☐　　　　　　*(1 mark)*

(b) ☐　　　　　　*(1 mark)*

(c) ☐　　　　　　*(1 mark)*

What I do to be 'green'

Class 8Y and the environment

37 Read about what class 8Y have done to help the environment this term.

Winter-Umweltsemester bei der Klasse 8Y

Wie viele Schüler und Schülerinnen haben Folgendes zu Hause gemacht?

29	Ich habe den Müll getrennt.
25	Ich bin zu Fuß oder mit dem Rad zur Schule gekommen.
20	Ich habe umweltfreundliche Produkte gekauft.
18	Ich war sparsam mit der Zentralheizung.
11	Ich habe mindestens eine Pfandflasche gekauft.
8	Ich habe Gartenabfälle kompostiert.
2	Ich habe Kleidung recycelt.

Write the correct number in the box for each action.

Example: Recycled clothes   2

(a) Bought a deposit bottle   ☐   *(1 mark)*

(b) Used environmentally friendly transport   ☐   *(1 mark)*

(c) Kept a compost bin   ☐   *(1 mark)*

(d) Turned the heating down   ☐   *(1 mark)*

Tobias and Maria

38 Listen to Tobias and Maria talking about how they help the environment.

(a) Complete the grid about Tobias's attempt to be environmentally friendly.

(i) Reason for visit to computer shop
.... *(1 mark)*
(ii) Tobias's problem when he tried to be environmentally friendly.
.... *(1 mark)*

(b) Complete the grid about Maria's attempt to be environmentally friendly.

(i) Reason for recycling clothes
.... *(1 mark)*
(ii) Objection to giving them to her cousins
.... *(1 mark)*

News headlines

In the news

39 Complete each of the following texts from a Swiss news site with one of the words which follows. Write the correct letter in the box.

(a)

Baum fällt auf der A1 bei Härkingen auf Auto

Ein Autofahrer hat bei einem Unfall auf der Autobahn A1 bei Härkingen großes Glück gehabt. Ein Baum ist am Donnerstagabend gegen die linke Seite des Autos gefallen. Der Autofahrer blieb [ ] und konnte das Auto problemlos durch die Beifahrertür verlassen.

A	schwer verletzt
B	unverletzt
C	in großer Gefahr

(1 mark)

(b)

Wetterphänomen „El Niño" kommt

Das weltweit gefährliche Wetterphänomen „El Niño" hat sich zurückgemeldet. Wissenschaftler meinen, dass diese gefürchtete Erwärmung der Wassertemperatur im tropischen Pazifik schlechtes Wetter und [ ] in unser Land bringen wird.

A	Straftaten
B	Stürme
C	Sonnenschein

(1 mark)

> Don't be put off by plural forms in texts – here *Stürme* is the plural of *Sturm* (storm).

(c)

Größter europäischer Jackpot sucht Gewinner

Der mit 190 Millionen Euro größte europäische Jackpot wird am Freitag Gewinner finden. Sollte niemand die fünf richtigen Zahlen und zwei Extrazahlen gewählt haben, wird man dem Gewinner die Rekordsumme das nächste Mal [ ].

A	zurücknehmen
B	vergessen
C	ausgeben

(1 mark)

(d)

Warnung vor einer neuen Lebensmittelkrise

Viele Hilfsorganisationen meinen, dass die Preise für Lebensmittel weltweit immer höher steigen. Sicher werden viele Menschen, besonders Frauen und Kinder, an Hungersnot leiden. Man bittet Sie jetzt, die Nummer 873 870 anzurufen, und der Kampagne Geld zu [ ]. Jeder Euro hilft!

A	spenden
B	ärgern
C	entscheiden

(1 mark)

(e)

Importprodukte in der Schweiz noch zu teuer

Für Schuhe, Kleider, Zeitschriften oder Kosmetikprodukte bezahlen Schweizer Kunden immer noch deutlich mehr als in den benachbarten [ ], wie Frankreich und Deutschland. So heißt es laut einer Umfrage dieser Zeitung.

A	Häusern
B	Ländern
C	Nachbarn

(1 mark)

Radio news

40 Listen to the news headlines. What exactly is each report about?

(a) .... *(1 mark)*

(b) .... *(1 mark)*

(c) .... *(1 mark)*

School subjects

My subjects

1 Read what these teenagers say about school subjects.

Murat: Ich finde Mathe sehr leicht.

Sara: Warum ist Englisch so langweilig?

Luisa: Mein Lieblingsfach ist Geschichte.

Hasan: Ich liebe Kunst, aber es ist schwer.

Anna: Montags haben wir Erdkunde. Fantastisch!

Johann: Ich mag Naturwissenschaften nicht.

Who mentions each subject? Write the initial of the person: **M** (Murat), **L** (Luisa), etc.

Example:

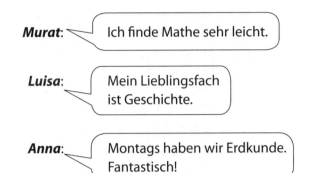

H

(a)

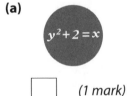

☐ *(1 mark)*

(b)

☐ *(1 mark)*

(c)

☐ *(1 mark)*

(d)

☐ *(1 mark)*

Subject likes and dislikes

2 Which subjects do these students mention? What do they think of them?

A	(atom)
B	(Africa)
C	(paintbrush)
D	$y^2 + 2 = x$
E	(flag)
F	(tools)
G	(Union Jack)

1	🙂
2	🙁
3	😐

Listen and write the correct letters and numbers in the boxes.

	Subject	Opinion
Example: Bierta	F	1
(a) Llayda			*(2 marks)*
(b) Celina			*(2 marks)*
(c) Romeo			*(2 marks)*
(d) Eva			*(2 marks)*

Opinions about school

Esma's school

3 Read what Esma says about her school.

> Meiner Meinung nach ist meine Gesamtschule toll und erfolgreich.
>
> Ich finde, dass es fair ist, wenn es in einer Schule viele Regeln gibt. Rauchen ist verboten und das finde ich gut. Aber ich finde es dumm, dass Kaugummis in Klassenzimmern verboten sind.

> Die Lehrer sind meistens nett, aber die Kunstlehrerin ist sehr streng und recht mies. Mein Lieblingsfach ist Geschichte und der Lehrer ist sehr lustig. Mathe finde ich ziemlich schwierig und ich habe immer Angst, wenn wir eine Klassenarbeit schreiben.
>
> Ich finde es ärgerlich, dass wir so viele Hausaufgaben bekommen. Manchmal haben wir Hausaufgaben in vier Fächern auf und das ist zu viel, meine ich. Nach der Schule tanze ich lieber oder ich spiele im Schulorchester. Hausaufgaben sind langweilig.

Write the correct letter in the box.

Example: Esma goes to a school which is …

A	successful
B	strict
C	terrible

A

> If you are not sure which answer is correct, try to decide which ones are definitely wrong.

(a) Esma thinks the rule about chewing gum is …

A	stupid
B	fair
C	good

☐   *(1 mark)*

(b) The Art teacher is …

A	friendly
B	horrible
C	funny

☐   *(1 mark)*

(c) In Maths Esma …

A	doesn't like tests
B	gets good marks
C	is in the top set

☐   *(1 mark)*

(d) After school Esma …

A	prefers to do homework
B	prefers to do dancing
C	has a piano lesson

☐   *(1 mark)*

My opinion on school

4 Listen to the pupils talking about their schools. What is their opinion of their school?

If positive, write **P**.

If negative, write **N**.

If positive and negative, write **P + N**.

> You are listening for the opinion of **school** – not just general opinions.

(a) David ☐   *(1 mark)*   **(c)** Marcel ☐   *(1 mark)*

(b) Jana ☐   *(1 mark)*   **(d)** Franka ☐   *(1 mark)*

School routine

Tom's school day

5 Read Tom's email about his school day.

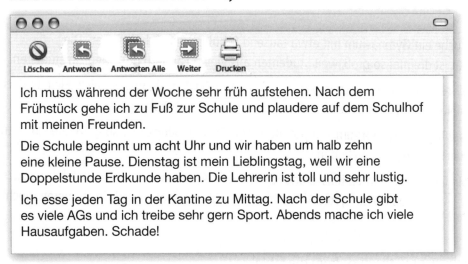

Löschen   Antworten   Antworten Alle   Weiter   Drucken

Ich muss während der Woche sehr früh aufstehen. Nach dem
Frühstück gehe ich zu Fuß zur Schule und plaudere auf dem Schulhof
mit meinen Freunden.

Die Schule beginnt um acht Uhr und wir haben um halb zehn
eine kleine Pause. Dienstag ist mein Lieblingstag, weil wir eine
Doppelstunde Erdkunde haben. Die Lehrerin ist toll und sehr lustig.

Ich esse jeden Tag in der Kantine zu Mittag. Nach der Schule gibt
es viele AGs und ich treibe sehr gern Sport. Abends mache ich viele
Hausaufgaben. Schade!

Which **four** statements are correct?

A	Tom gets up early.
B	Tom walks to school.
C	Tom chats to friends on the way.
D	School starts at 08.00.
E	The morning break is at 10.30.

F	Tom loves Tuesdays.
G	The geography teacher is strict.
H	Tom has lunch in the canteen.
I	Tom doesn't get much homework.

Example: A

Write the **four** correct letters in the boxes. ☐ ☐ ☐ ☐   *(4 marks)*

Around school

6 Listen to these pupils at school. Where are they going?

A   **B**   **C**   **D**

 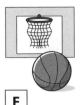 

E   **F**   **G**

Write the correct letter in the box.

Example: D

(a) ☐ *(1 mark)*   **(b)** ☐ *(1 mark)*   **(c)** ☐ *(1 mark)*   **(d)** ☐ *(1 mark)*

German schools

Max's schools

7 Read Max's text about schools.

Ich besuche ein Gymnasium mit etwa tausend Schülern und Schülerinnen. Die ☐ nebenan ist dreimal so groß, weil Studenten aus vielen Ländern dort Medizin studieren.

Als kleines Kind war ich auch in der ☐ sehr glücklich. Sie war ziemlich klein und ich hatte viele Freunde, mit denen ich den ganzen Tag gespielt habe.

Der erste Tag am Gymnasium war furchtbar. Das Schulgebäude war so groß und ich konnte nicht das richtige ☐ finden.

Jetzt bin ich in der zehnten Klasse und ich finde die Arbeit ziemlich schwer. Ich brauche sehr gute ☐ , weil ich ein gutes Abitur machen will und später Medizin studieren möchte.

Complete the gaps with words from the table.

A	Uni
B	Regeln
C	Realschule
D	Klassenzimmer
E	Noten
F	Fabrik
G	Grundschule
H	Zeugnis

> If you are not sure of the answer, eliminate the words you know make no sense or have already been chosen, before using intelligent guesswork to get to the correct answer.

(4 marks)

An English school

8 Listen to Aylin describing her new school.

(a) What did Aylin particularly like about her school in Germany? Give **two** details.

(i) .... *(1 mark)*

(ii) .... *(1 mark)*

(b) What does she think about her new school?

(i) Positive: .... *(1 mark)*

(ii) Negative: .... *(1 mark)*

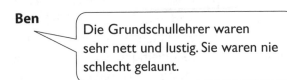

Primary school

Primary school memories

9 What do these people remember about primary school?

Ben
Die Grundschullehrer waren sehr nett und lustig. Sie waren nie schlecht gelaunt.

Tom
Es war besser, weil wir keine Hausaufgaben machen mussten. Nach der Schule konnten wir Fußball spielen.

Lena
Ich fand die Grundschule ziemlich langweilig und ich war froh, als ich zur Hauptschule gegangen bin.

Susi
Die Grundschule war toll, weil ich oft gezeichnet habe. Ich hatte eine große Federmappe mit vielen bunten Filzstiften und Bleistiften. Kunst ist immer noch mein Lieblingsfach.

Eric
In der Grundschule gab es keinen Stress, weil wir keinen Stundenplan hatten. Jeden Tag hat es Spaß gemacht!

Jens
In der Grundschule konnte man stundenlang auf dem Schulhof spielen. Das war super klasse.

Complete the table by writing the correct letter.

A   **B**   **C**

D   **E**   **F**

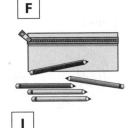

G   **H**   **I**

Ben	
Tom	
Lena	
Susi	
Eric	
Jens	

(6 marks)

Primary school highlights

10 Listen to Knut, Hannes and Petra talking about their primary school highlights. What do they think?

A	'I used to love feeding the ducks.'		**D**	'I prefer art lessons now.'
B	'It was a shame we didn't sing more.'		**E**	'I hated having to eat fruit.'
C	'I loved all my felt tip pens.'		**F**	'I dreaded the swimming lesson.'

Write the correct letter in the box.

(a) Knut ☐ *(1 mark)*   **(b)** Hannes ☐ *(1 mark)*   **(c)** Petra ☐ *(1 mark)*

Rules at school

B READING

Notices in school

11 Fill the gaps with a word from the list below. Write the correct letter in the box.

(a) Ich weiß, dass man im Klassenzimmer keine Handys benutzen darf, aber gestern musste ich dringend meiner Mutter etwas Wichtiges ⬚, also habe ich ihr eine SMS geschickt. In diesem Moment hat die Lateinlehrerin mich angesehen …

A	vergessen
B	ausrichten
C	anrufen

(1 mark)

(b) Man kann die Schule erst mit achtzehn Jahren verlassen und das finde ich schade, weil viele Jugendlichen lieber mit sechzehn Jahren eine Arbeitsstelle bekommen würden. Aber das ⬚ erlaubt ihnen das nicht.

A	Fach
B	Geld
C	Gesetz

(1 mark)

(c) Unsere Schulregeln finde ich recht mies und ungerecht, aber ich komme täglich pünktlich in die Schule und mache rechtzeitig meine Hausaufgaben, weil ich immer Angst habe, dass ich sonst ⬚ muss.

A	abschreiben
B	nachsitzen
C	schwänzen

(1 mark)

(d) An unserer Schule ist der Direktor gar nicht streng und es herrscht oft Unruhe im Klassenzimmer, weil manche Schüler sich so schlecht benehmen. Viele Schüler machen zwei-oder dreimal in der Woche blau – obwohl sie ⬚ sind, bekommen sie dafür keine Strafarbeit.

A	abwesend
B	anwesend
C	unpünktlich

(1 mark)

> First, eliminate any answer options that you know to be incorrect.

E LISTENING   67

School issues

12 Listen to the school rules.

 **A**

  B

  C

 **D**

  E

  F

 **G**

Which rule is it? Write the correct letter in the box.

Example: A

(a) ⬚ *(1 mark)* **(b)** ⬚ *(1 mark)* **(c)** ⬚ *(1 mark)* **(d)** ⬚ *(1 mark)*

School problems

Pressures

13 These young people are writing about their dislikes at school.

Bernadette — In der Kantine ist es immer sehr laut.

Rene — Ich finde den Direktor zu streng.

Dominik — Ich habe Angst vor den Prüfungen.

Nina — Ich habe keine Freunde.

Marlene — Ich verstehe die Hausaufgaben nicht.

Andela — Ich bleibe lieber zu Hause.

Pan — Ich habe Probleme in Geschichte.

Write the initial of the person: **B** (Bernadette), **R** (Rene), etc.

Example: Who hasn't made friends?   N

Who ...

(a) finds history difficult? ☐   *(1 mark)*

(b) has difficulty with homework? ☐   *(1 mark)*

(c) worries about exams? ☐   *(1 mark)*

(d) finds the headteacher too strict? ☐   *(1 mark)*

Thoughts on schooling

14 Listen to what these people think about school.

Write **P** for positive.

Write **N** for negative.

Write **P + N** for positive and negative.

(a) ☐   *(1 mark)*

(b) ☐   *(1 mark)*

(c) ☐   *(1 mark)*

(d) ☐   *(1 mark)*

Future education plans

Future plans

15 You read this email from Melissa.

Löschen   Antworten   Antworten Alle   Weiter   Drucken

Hallo Laura,

gestern habe ich die letzte Prüfung für die Mittlere Reife geschrieben und ich bin jetzt wegen der Ergebnisse sehr nervös! Ich brauche nämlich ausgezeichnete Noten, um auf das beste Gymnasium der Gegend zu gehen.

Bevor das nächste Semester anfängt, will ich unbedingt mit Freunden nach Spanien fliegen. Wir wollen uns alle richtig ausruhen, damit wir im September bereit sind, wieder fleißig zu arbeiten.

Als ich jünger war, wollte ich Krankenschwester werden, aber jetzt denke ich anders. Letztes Jahr fand ich das Arbeitspraktikum bei einem Tierarzt so faszinierend, dass ich mich entschieden habe, lieber mit Tieren als mit Menschen zu arbeiten.

Nach der Schule ist es mein Traum, an der Uni Tiermedizin zu studieren. Das Studium wird einige Jahre dauern, und obwohl es billiger wäre, als Studentin noch zu Hause zu wohnen, will ich lieber in eine andere Stadt ziehen. So werde ich sicher neue Erfahrungen machen und ich halte es für wichtig, selbstständig zu werden.

Also, schöne Ferien!

Tschüs

Melissa

(a) What did Melissa do yesterday?

.... *(1 mark)*

(b) Why exactly is Melissa nervous?

.... *(1 mark)*

(c) Why do she and her friends need to go to relax in Spain?

.... *(1 mark)*

(d) How did work experience influence her?

.... *(1 mark)*

(e) What does Melissa want to do at university?

.... *(1 mark)*

(f) Why does Melissa want to study away from home?

.... *(1 mark)*

Future careers

Future options

16 You read this article.

> Es ist heute bei der Jugend nicht mehr so beliebt, auf ein Gymnasium und dann auf die Uni zu gehen. Viele Schüler bevorzugen einen Ausbildungsplatz als Friseur oder Klempner. Sie finden es attraktiv, weil sie dann gleich ein bisschen Geld verdienen und sich auch auf die Zukunft vorbereiten. Ein Lehrling meinte: „Wenn ich später Kinder habe, möchte ich halbtags in einem Friseursalon arbeiten." Einige junge Leute studieren jedoch an der Uni, um in Zukunft einen guten Beruf mit hohem Gehalt zu haben. Ihre Hoffnung ist es, einen tollen Lebensstil mit einem schnellen Auto und einer großen Eigentumswohnung zu haben. Es gibt eine große Auswahl an Berufen, die geeignet für die Schüler sind, aber man muss nach ihnen suchen. Manche Schüler wollen Briefträger oder Gärtner werden und sie meinen, dass sie auch im Winter oder bei schlechtem Wetter lieber im Freien als in einem Gebäude mit Klimaanlage arbeiten. Beim Arbeitsamt finden sie genau solche Stellen. Nach dem Abitur arbeiten manche Schüler freiwillig bei einer Wohltätigkeitsorganisation. Sie helfen vielleicht in einem Heim für Obdachlose oder alten Menschen, und lernen dabei vieles. Ein freiwilliger Mitarbeiter bei einem Frühstücksklub für Kinder meinte: „Ich möchte eventuell in einer Grundschule unterrichten und möchte zuerst ein bisschen etwas über Kinder erfahren, bevor ich auf die Uni in Berlin gehe."

Read the following sentences. Write **T** (True), **F** (False) or **?** (Not in the text) in the box.

Example: As many students today choose university as previously.   F

(a) Apprenticeships prepare you better for the future than university.   ☐   *(1 mark)*

(b) You can choose to do an apprenticeship as a plumber.   ☐   *(1 mark)*

(c) Hairdressing apprenticeships are part time.   ☐   *(1 mark)*

(d) University courses offer the hope of good pay in the future.   ☐   *(1 mark)*

(e) The lifestyle at university is amazing.   ☐   *(1 mark)*

(f) There is not a great variety of jobs available.   ☐   *(1 mark)*

(g) Some people enjoy working outside whatever the weather.   ☐   *(1 mark)*

(h) Some school leavers do voluntary work with refugees.   ☐   *(1 mark)*

(i) To be a teacher, the volunteer has to work with children before starting his course.   ☐   *(1 mark)*

> Don't mistake a False answer (**F**) with a Not in the text answer (**?**). If you can't find any reference to the statement in the text, the chances are it is not there, so the answer is (**?**).

Had a go ☐   Nearly there ☐   Nailed it! ☐

Jobs

E

Who wants to be what?

17 Read about what these people want to be.

Christian — Ich möchte gern mit Kindern arbeiten, also werde ich Lehrer.

Bettina — Ich werde auf jeden Fall bei einer Tierarzt-Praxis als Tierärztin arbeiten.

Hugo — Mein Traum ist es, Feuerwehrmann zu werden.

Ellie — Ich glaube, dass ich Polizistin werde.

Paul — Ich habe keine Ahnung. Vielleicht Klempner?

> You only have to look for the job word each time – you don't have to understand everything else.

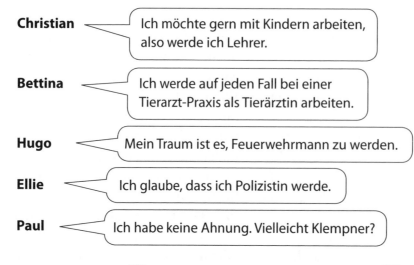    

A   B   C   D   E   F   G

What job do they want? Complete the table by writing the correct letter.

Example: Christian	C
Bettina	
Hugo	
Ellie	
Paul	

(1 mark)
(1 mark)
(1 mark)
(1 mark)

D

Jobs

18 Listen to five people talking about their jobs.

Example: What job does Silas have? ..... *policeman* ....

(a) What does Phillipa think of her job?

.... *(1 mark)*

(b) Why did Özlem want to be a vet?

.... *(1 mark)*

(c) Why has Christina gone back to school?

.... *(1 mark)*

(d) Why has Gerhard become a butcher?

.... *(1 mark)*

Job adverts

C

Job adverts

19 You read this advertisement in a restaurant window.

— KELLNER GESUCHT —

Bewerben Sie sich heute um eine Stelle bei uns!

Sind Sie fleißig und freundlich? Möchten Sie in einem modernen Restaurant mit tollen Kollegen und unter guten Arbeitsbedingungen arbeiten?

Wir suchen Kellner/innen für unser neu eröffnetes italienisches Restaurant am Dom.

Die erfolgreichen Kandidaten werden 8,50 € pro Stunde bekommen.

Wir sind stolz auf unseren internationalen Restaurantbetrieb und wir bieten allen Angestellten ausgezeichnete Aufstiegschancen an.

Kommen Sie heute vorbei, um das Bewerbungsformular abzuholen. Schicken Sie uns das Formular mit Lebenslauf spätestens bis Montag, den 12. März, wieder zurück.

(a) What is the advert asking you to do?

.... *(1 mark)*

(b) Mention **two** ways the restaurant makes itself seem a good place to work.

(i) .... *(1 mark)*

(ii) .... *(1 mark)*

(c) What else are you told about the restaurant? Mention **two** details.

(i) .... *(1 mark)*

(ii) .... *(1 mark)*

(d) What do you have to do if you are interested in the job?

.... *(1 mark)*

B

A job advert

20 Listen to Lars talking about a job advert he has seen.

A	boring	D	his mother's office	G	good
B	really terrible	E	the cinema	H	not perfect
C	the youth club	F	the travel agency	I	the sports centre

Write the correct letter in the box to complete the sentences.

Example: The job is in ☐ F ☐ .

(a) Lars has worked in ☐ *(1 mark)*

(b) Lars thinks office work is ☐ *(1 mark)*

(c) He thinks the hours of the Saturday job are ☐ *(1 mark)*

(d) On Saturday evenings Lars likes to go to ☐ or ☐ . *(2 marks)*

CV

D

Leni's CV

21 You read Leni's CV.

LEBENSLAUF

Name: Leni Weigel

Geburtsdatum:
Ich bin am 2. April 1995 in Frankfurt geboren.

Schule:
Zurzeit besuche ich eine Gesamtschule und bekomme gute Noten und Zeugnisse. Mein Lieblingsfach ist Chemie und ich mag auch Geschichte.

Arbeitserfahrung:
Samstags und sonntags arbeite ich als Kellnerin in einem Café und ich finde die Arbeit interessant.

Interessen:
Ich habe viele Hobbys, aber am liebsten tanze ich. Ich gehe zweimal pro Woche in eine Tanzschule. Früher habe ich gern Tischtennis gespielt, aber jetzt nicht mehr.

Zukunftspläne:
In Zukunft möchte ich Mechanikerin werden.

Which **four** items are relevant to Leni? Write the **four** correct letters in the boxes.

Example:

F ☐ ☐ ☐ ☐

(4 marks)

E

Martha's CV

22 Listen to Martha talking about her CV.

Complete Martha's CV.

Example: Surname:	Wolf
(a) Date of birth:	*(1 mark)*
(b) Type of school:	*(1 mark)*
(c) Work experience:	*(1 mark)*
(d) Interests (mention one):	*(1 mark)*

Job application

Hannah's application letter

23 Read Hannah's application letter for a job.

> Sehr geehrte Frau Braun,
>
> in den Sommerferien möchte ich im Segelklub arbeiten, weil ich gern ☐ mache und ich gut mit anderen Leuten auskomme. Ich kann am 7. Juli anfangen und am liebsten würde ich vier Wochen lang arbeiten.
>
> Ich habe ein Jahr in London gewohnt und spreche gut Englisch. Ich lerne seit einem Jahr in der Schule auch Spanisch und ich glaube, dass meine Sprachkenntnisse sehr ☐ sein werden.
>
> Letzten August habe ich drei Wochen lang als ☐ in einem Kaufhaus in der Stadtmitte gearbeitet und, obwohl ich das sehr interessant fand, arbeite ich lieber im Freien.
>
> Ich hoffe, später Fremdsprachen zu ☐ und dann in Spanien oder England zu arbeiten.
>
> Mit freundlichen Grüßen
>
> Ihre
>
> Hannah Schulz

> Make sure you revise all tenses to help you understand texts like this more easily.

Fill in the gaps in the text with words from the table. Write the correct letter in the box.

A	Verkäuferin
B	Wassersport
C	freundlich

D	Bäuerin
E	vermeiden
F	nützlich

G	Radtouren
H	studieren

(4 marks)

Job application

24 Listen to Martin and Johanna discussing an interview.

(a) What has Johanna forgotten? Write the correct letter in the box.

A    B   C

☐ *(1 mark)*

(b) What time is the interview?

.... *(1 mark)*

(c) How do you have to look to get a job, according to Johanna?

.... *(1 mark)*

(d) Where has Johanna left something?

.... *(1 mark)*

79

Job interview

Interview extracts

25 Read these extracts from job interviews.

(a)

> „Ich möchte dieses Jahr nach Berlin fahren, um einen Deutschkurs zu machen."

(i) Why does this person want to spend time in Berlin?

.... *(1 mark)*

(ii) When does this person want to go?

.... *(1 mark)*

(b)

> „Ich komme gut mit anderen Menschen aus – ich bin hilfsbereit und freundlich."

What positive attributes does this person have? Mention **two** of them.

(i) .... *(1 mark)*

(ii) .... *(1 mark)*

Being interviewed for a job

26 Listen to Sebastian's job interview. Write the correct letter in the box.

(a) Which task **doesn't** Sebastian mention?

A	waiting at table
B	washing up
C	night porter

☐   *(1 mark)*

(b) What is Sebastian's opinion of his last summer job?

A	positive
B	positive and negative
C	negative

☐   *(1 mark)*

(c) What was the guests' general opinion of the other hotel staff?

A	helpful
B	unhelpful
C	efficient

☐   *(1 mark)*

(d) Why does Sebastian want to travel?

A	he doesn't know anything about other countries
B	he wants to learn a new language
C	he thinks he will have a better chance of getting a job

☐   *(1 mark)*

(e) What other reason does he give for travelling?

A	he enjoyed the experience last time
B	to improve his CV
C	to meet potential employers

☐   *(1 mark)*

Opinions about jobs

Views on jobs

27 Read Susi and Elif's views on their jobs.

> **Susi**: Ich glaube, dass es nicht notwendig ist, einen hohen Lohn zu verdienen. Viel wichtiger ist es, einen fairen und netten Chef zu haben. Ich komme mit den anderen Arbeitern in der Fabrik sehr gut aus, aber die Chefin geht uns allen auf die Nerven und sie ist ziemlich gemein. Ehrlich gesagt würde ich lieber weniger Geld verdienen und bessere Arbeitsbedingungen haben. Trotzdem bin ich froh, dass ich berufstätig bin und dass die Arbeitsstunden nicht zu lang sind.

> **Elif**: Ich finde meinen Job sehr schwer, weil ich von 23:00 bis 06:00 Uhr Schichtarbeit machen muss. Ich arbeite bei der Post und obwohl das eine sehr gute Erfahrung ist und die Mitarbeiter nett sind, ist es nicht mein Traumjob. Ich möchte viel lieber in einer Fabrik oder in einem Büro arbeiten, wo man zumindest normale Arbeitsstunden hätte. Der einzige Vorteil ist, dass die Arbeit gut bezahlt ist und das ist mir wichtig, weil ich auf ein neues Auto spare.

Who do the following statements apply to?

If the statement applies only to Susi write **S**.

If the statement applies only to Elif write **E**.

If the statement applies to both Susi and Elif write **S + E**.

(a) I like my working hours. ☐ *(1 mark)*

(b) I would like to work in a factory. ☐ *(1 mark)*

(c) I get on well with my colleagues. ☐ *(1 mark)*

(d) My wages make up for other disadvantages. ☐ *(1 mark)*

A new job

28 Listen to Ben talking about his first day at work.

(a) What was Ben's task on his first day at work?

.... *(1 mark)*

(b) What did the boss often do in front of the customers?

.... *(1 mark)*

(c) Why would Ben recommend working at the department store? Give **two** reasons.

(i) .... *(1 mark)*

(ii) .... *(1 mark)*

Part-time work

Jobs for teenagers

29 You see this article about part-time jobs.

> **Mina (14)** trägt jeden Tag Zeitungen aus, aber sie findet es recht schwer, weil sie so früh aufstehen muss. Sie ist ein Nachtmensch! Warum macht sie das also? Sie braucht das Geld für den Sommerurlaub.
>
> **Samstags ist Felix (18)** bei der Arbeit in einem Supermarkt zu finden. Es macht ihm viel Spaß, obwohl er abends sehr müde ist, weil die Arbeitsstunden lang sind. Das Beste ist, wenn er an der Kasse arbeiten kann, weil er sehr gern mit den Kunden spricht.
>
> **Mehmet (17)** hilft seinem Onkel, der ein türkisches Restaurant in der Stadtmitte besitzt. Am Anfang musste er das Geschirr abwaschen, aber jetzt darf er als Kellner arbeiten und das findet er viel interessanter, obwohl die Kunden ihm manchmal auf die Nerven gehen.
>
> **Hannah (16)** arbeitet am Wochenende mit ihrer Mutter, die Gärtnerin ist. Hannah macht das freiwillig, weil sie gern im Freien ist und es langweilig findet, alleine zu Hause zu sein. Außerdem will sie später auch einmal Gärtnerin werden.

> Don't make your answer so brief that you miss out on including the relevant detail to score the mark.

(a) What is Mina's job?

.... *(1 mark)*

(b) What doesn't she like about it?

.... *(1 mark)*

(c) What is the disadvantage of Felix's job?

.... *(1 mark)*

(d) Which task does he most enjoy?

.... *(1 mark)*

(e) Where does Mehmet work?

.... *(1 mark)*

(f) Why is the job more interesting now?

.... *(1 mark)*

(g) What does Hannah like about her job?

.... *(1 mark)*

(h) Why is the work good experience for her?

.... *(1 mark)*

Work experience

Work experience blog

30 Read Emine's blog about work experience.

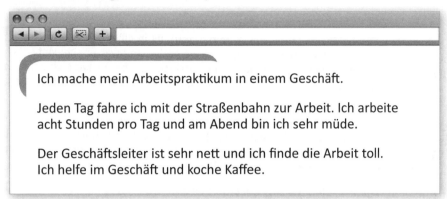

Ich mache mein Arbeitspraktikum in einem Geschäft.

Jeden Tag fahre ich mit der Straßenbahn zur Arbeit. Ich arbeite acht Stunden pro Tag und am Abend bin ich sehr müde.

Der Geschäftsleiter ist sehr nett und ich finde die Arbeit toll. Ich helfe im Geschäft und koche Kaffee.

> Write in **English**. Answers in German will gain no marks.

(a) Where is Emine working? Write the correct letter in the box.

A  B  C

☐ *(1 mark)*

(b) How many hours does Emine work per day? .... *(1 mark)*

(c) What is the manager like? .... *(1 mark)*

(d) What does Emine think of the work? Write the correct letter in the box.

A   B   C

☐ *(1 mark)*

Sol and Anita's work experience

31 Listen to Sol and Anita talking about their work experience. Write the correct letter in the box.

> Don't just listen for key words – you need to understand what is being said about the key words to identify the answers.

(a) Sol didn't enjoy his work experience because of …

A	the location
B	the clothes he had to wear
C	the customers

☐ *(1 mark)*

(b) In future he would like to work …

A	in an office
B	in a shop
C	in the town centre

☐ *(1 mark)*

(c) Anita didn't enjoy her work experience because …

A	the children were badly behaved
B	it wasn't varied enough
C	her boss was impatient with her

☐ *(1 mark)*

(d) Anita found her work experience …

A	worthwhile
B	interesting
C	fun

☐ *(1 mark)*

My work experience

Lukas's work experience

32 You read this article.

> Letzten Monat hat der sechzehnjährige Lukas ein Arbeitspraktikum in einer Autofabrik gemacht. Am Ende meinte er, dass es eine tolle Erfahrung war, aber am ersten Tag war er schlecht gelaunt, weil er nur Akten sortieren und Telefonanrufe beantworten durfte. Er hat sich dabei sehr gelangweilt, weil er nicht ein einziges Auto gesehen hatte und er kehrte am Abend sehr enttäuscht nach Hause zurück.
>
> In den nächsten acht Tagen wurde die Arbeit viel interessanter, weil Lukas in der Werkstatt arbeiten durfte. Lukas berichtete abends im Blog: „Es war unglaublich! Hunderte von Autos auf einem langen Fließband!" Weil seine Kollegen sehr freundlich und geduldig waren, hat Lukas recht viel gelernt und er hat sich entschieden, später unbedingt Automechaniker zu werden.
>
> Der Höhepunkt kam für Lukas am letzten Tag, als er mit dem Chef zur Messe fuhr. Er sagte: „Ich fand es höchst interessant, mit den Vertretern zu sprechen. Sie waren sehr hilfsbereit und der Chef hat mir auch viele Ratschläge gegeben."
>
> Der Chef, Herr Lehmann, sagte: „Lukas war ein sehr fleißiger und begeisterter Schüler, dem wir gerne in Zukunft eine Stelle hier bei uns anbieten würden."

Read the following sentences. Write **T** (True), **F** (False) or **?** (Not in the text) in the box.

(a) Lukas found the office work both positive and negative. ☐ *(1 mark)*

(b) Lukas was disappointed after his first day. ☐ *(1 mark)*

(c) Working in the factory was noisy. ☐ *(1 mark)*

(d) Lukas preferred working in the factory to working in the office. ☐ *(1 mark)*

(e) Lukas enjoyed meeting sales staff at the meeting. ☐ *(1 mark)*

(f) Lukas's boss earned a lot of money. ☐ *(1 mark)*

(g) Lukas made a good impression on his boss. ☐ *(1 mark)*

(h) Lukas has been offered a job with the firm. ☐ *(1 mark)*

A new job

33 Listen to these people talking about their work experience.

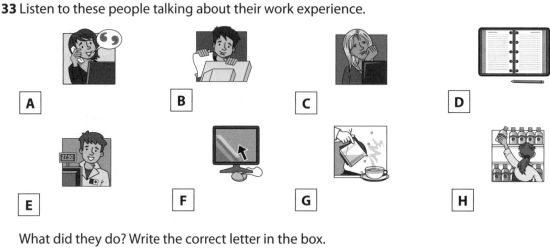

What did they do? Write the correct letter in the box.

(a) ☐ *(1 mark)*   **(b)** ☐ *(1 mark)*   **(c)** ☐ *(1 mark)*   **(d)** ☐ *(1 mark)*

Gender and plurals

In the nominative, German nouns are either **der** (masculine), **die** (feminine) or **das** (neuter).
der / **die** / **das** = the

der Hund   **die** Katze   **das** Pferd

A Put a circle round the correct article.

1 der / die / das Mülleimer (*m.*)

2 der / die / das Kino (*n.*)

3 der / die / das Krankenschwester (*f.*)

4 der / die / das Rucksack (*m.*)

5 der / die / das Handy (*n.*)

6 der / die / das Restaurant (*n.*)

7 der / die / das Autobahn (*f.*)

8 der / die / das Sportlehrer (*m.*)

9 der / die / das Umwelt (*f.*)

B Complete with **der**, **die** or **das**.

1 .... Haus ist modern. (*n.*)

2 .... Schüler heißt Max. (*m.*)

3 .... Schülerin heißt Demet. (*f.*)

4 .... Computer ist kaputt. (*m.*)

5 .... Zug fährt langsam. (*m.*)

6 .... Sparkasse ist geschlossen. (*f.*)

7 .... Zeitung kostet 1 Euro. (*f.*)

8 .... Buch ist langweilig. (*n.*)

In the accusative, the article **der** changes to **den** (masculine), but **die** and **das** don't change.

	m.	*f.*	*n.*	*pl.*
Accusative	**den**	die	das	die

Wir mögen **den** Sportlehrer.

C Write in **den**, **die** or **das**.

1 Wir haben .... Pizza gegessen. (*f.*)

2 Wir können .... Krankenhaus sehen. (*n.*)

3 Ich mache .... Hausaufgaben. (*fpl.*)

4 Vati kauft .... Pullover. (*m.*)

5 Liest du .... Buch? (*n.*)

6 Ich mähe .... Rasen. (*m.*)

German plurals come in many forms. The most common ones are **–e** and **–n**, but many are irregular, maybe adding an umlaut or simply staying the same.

(S) Brief   ⟶   (P) Brief**e**
(S) Tasse   ⟶   (P) Tasse**n**
(S) Teller   ⟶   (P) Teller
(S) Glas   ⟶   (P) Gl**ä**s**er**

D Write **S** if the noun is singular and **P** if it is plural. If it could be either, put **E**.

Haus ...., Buch ...., Männer ...., Autos ...., Häuser ...., Supermarkt ....,

Tisch ...., Mann ...., Supermärkte ...., Tische ...., Handys ....,

Zimmer ...., Bilder ...., Computer ....

Cases 1

> The prepositions which trigger a change to the accusative are **für**, **um**, **durch**, **gegen**, **bis** and **ohne**.
>
> | | m. | f. | n. | pl. |
> |---|---|---|---|---|
> | **Nominative** | der | die | das | die |
> | **Accusative** | de**n** | die | das | die |
> | | | | | |
> | **Nominative** | ein | eine | ein | keine |
> | **Accusative** | ein**en** | eine | ein | keine |

A Write in **den**, **die**, **das**, **einen**, **eine** or **ein**.

1 um .... Ecke (*round the corner*) (*f.*)

2 durch .... Stadt (*through the town*) (*f.*)

3 ohne .... Auto (*without a car*) (*n.*)

4 für .... Schule (*for the school*) (*f.*)

5 für .... Freund (*for a friend*) (*m.*)

6 gegen .... Wand (*against the wall*) (*f.*)

7 durch .... Wald (*through a wood*) (*m.*)

> The prepositions which trigger a change to the dative are: **aus**, **außer**, **bei**, **gegenüber**, **mit**, **nach**, **seit**, **von** and **zu**.
>
> | | m. | f. | n. | pl. |
> |---|---|---|---|---|
> | **Nominative** | der | die | das | die |
> | **Dative** | de**m** | de**r** | de**m** | de**n** |
> | | | | | |
> | **Nominative** | ein | eine | ein | keine |
> | **Dative** | ein**em** | ein**er** | ein**em** | keine**n** |

B Write in **dem**, **der**, **einem** or **einer**.

1 mit .... Bus (*by bus*) (*m.*)

2 seit .... Sommer (*since the summer*) (*m.*)

3 zu .... Bank (*to the bank*) (*f.*)

4 nach .... Party (*after the party*) (*f.*)

5 bei .... Freund (*at a friend's house*) (*m.*)

6 von .... Onkel (*from an uncle*) (*m.*)

7 gegenüber .... Tankstelle (*opposite the petrol station*) (*f.*)

8 außer .... Lehrerin (*apart from the teacher*) (*f.*)

> A few prepositions trigger a change to the genitive: **während**, **trotz** and **wegen**.
>
> | | m. | f. | n. | pl. |
> |---|---|---|---|---|
> | **Nominative** | der | die | das | die |
> | **Genitive** | de**s** | de**r** | de**s** | de**r** |
> | | | | | |
> | **Nominative** | ein | eine | ein | keine |
> | **Genitive** | ein**es** | ein**er** | ein**es** | keine**n** |

C Write in **der** or **des**.

1 wegen .... Wetters (*because of the weather*) (*n.*)

2 während .... Stunde (*during the lesson*) (*f.*)

3 trotz .... Regens (*despite the rain*) (*m.*)

Cases 2

> These prepositions trigger a change to the accusative if there is movement towards a place, or the dative if there is no movement:
>
> | *an* (on, at) | *auf* (on) | *hinter* (behind) |
> |---|---|---|
> | *in* (in) | *neben* (next to) | *über* (over, above) |
> | *unter* (under) | *vor* (in front of) | *zwischen* (between) |
>
> See page 86 for the accusative and dative forms of articles.

A Circle the correct article.

1 Wir fahren in **der** / **die** Stadt. (f.)

2 Meine Schwester ist in **der** / **die** Schule. (f.)

3 Das Essen steht auf **den** / **dem** Tisch. (m.)

4 Ich steige auf **die** / **der** Mauer. (f.)

5 Wir hängen das Bild an **der** / **die** Wand. (f.)

6 Jetzt ist das Bild an **der** / **die** Wand. (f.)

7 Die Katze läuft hinter **einen** / **einem** Schrank. (m.)

8 Wo ist die Katze jetzt? Hinter **den** / **dem** Schrank. (m.)

9 Die Bäckerei steht zwischen **einem** / **einen** Supermarkt (m.) und **einer** / **eine** Post. (f.)

10 Das Flugzeug fliegt über **die** / **der** Stadt. (f.)

11 Ich stelle die Flaschen in **dem** / **den** Schrank. (m.)

12 Der Bus steht an **der** / **die** Haltestelle. (f.)

> Some verbs work with a preposition which is followed by the accusative.

B Circle the correct article. Then translate the sentences into English.

1 Die Kinder streiten sich über **das** / **dem** Fernsehprogramm. (*n.*)

2 Wir freuen uns auf **das** / **dem** Fest. (*n.*)

3 Ich ärgere mich oft über **der** / **die** Arbeit. (*f.*)

4 Martin hat sich an **der** / **die** Sonne gewöhnt. (*f.*)

5 Wie lange warten Sie auf **der** / **die** Straßenbahn? (*f.*)

1 ....

2 ....

3 ....

4 ....

5 ....

> Certain special phrases have a preposition followed by either the accusative or the dative. You have to learn these.

C Draw lines to link the German and English phrases.

1 auf dem Land	*on the internet*
2 vor allem	*on the right*
3 auf die Nerven	*in the country*
4 auf der rechten Seite	*on my nerves*
5 im Internet	*above all*

Cases 3

> **Dieser** (this) and **jener** (that) follow the pattern of **der, die, das**.
>
> | | **m.** | **f.** | **n.** | **pl.** |
> |---|---|---|---|---|
> | **Nominative** | dieser | diese | dieses | diese |
> | **Accusative** | diese**n** | diese | dieses | diese |
> | **Dative** | diese**m** | diese**r** | diese**m** | diese**n** |

A Add the endings.

1 *this man*   dies........ Mann (*m.*)

2 *with this man*   mit dies........ Mann (*m.*)

3 *this woman*   dies........ Frau (*f.*)

4 *for this woman*   für dies........ Frau (*f.*)

5 *that horse*   jen........ Pferd (*n.*)

6 *on that horse*   auf jen........ Pferd (*n.*)

> **Kein, mein, dein, sein, ihr, unser, euer (eure)** and **Ihr** follow the pattern of **ein**.
>
> | | **m.** | **f.** | **n.** | **pl.** |
> |---|---|---|---|---|
> | **Nominative** | kein | keine | kein | keine |
> | **Accusative** | kein**en** | keine | kein | keine |
> | **Dative** | kein**em** | kein**er** | kein**em** | kein**en** |

B Complete the words where necessary with the correct ending.

1 Unser........ Schwester heißt Monika. (*f.*)

2 Ich habe kein........ Bruder. (*m.*)

3 Mein........ Schule ist nicht sehr groß. (*f.*)

4 Hast du dein........ Laptop vergessen? (*m.*)

5 Wie ist Ihr........ Name, bitte? (*m.*)

6 Meine Lehrerin hat ihr........ Schulbücher nicht mit. (*pl.*)

7 Wo steht Ihr........ Auto? (*n.*)

8 Wir arbeiten in unser........ Büro. (*n.*)

9 Wo ist euer........ Wohnung? (*f.*)

10 Mein........ Lieblingsfächer sind Mathe und Informatik. (*pl.*)

11 Wie heißt dein........ Freundin? (*f.*)

12 Leider haben wir kein........ Zeit. (*f.*)

13 Ihr........ E-Mail war nicht sehr höflich. (*f.*)

14 Olaf geht mit sein........ Freund spazieren. (*m.*)

15 Madonna singt ihr........ besten Hits. (*pl.*)

16 Wo habt ihr euer........ Auto stehen lassen? (*n.*)

Specials

17 Ich habe .... Ahnung. (*I've no idea.*) (*f.*)

18 Ich habe .... Lust. (*I don't want to.*) (*f.*)

19 Das war .... Fehler. (*That was my mistake.*) (*m.*)

20 .... Meinung nach ... (*In my opinion ...*) (*f.*)

Adjective endings

Adjectives after the definite article end in either **-e** or **-en**.

	m.	**f.**	**n.**	**pl.**
Nominative	der klein**e** Hund	die klein**e** Maus	das klein**e** Haus	die klein**en** Kinder
Accusative	den klein**en** Hund	die klein**e** Maus	das klein**e** Haus	die klein**en** Kinder
Dative	dem klein**en** Hund	der klein**en** Maus	dem klein**en** Haus	den klein**en** Kinder**n**

A Fill the gaps with the suggested adjective and its correct ending.

1 Die .... Schülerin bekommt gute Noten. (*f.*, intelligent__)

2 Wir fahren mit dem .... Bus in die Stadt. (*m.*, nächst__)

3 Hast du den .... Vogel gesehen? (*m.*, gelb__)

4 Der .... Lehrer ist streng. (*m.*, altmodisch__)

5 Ich kaufe dieses .... Kleid. (*n.*, schwarz__)

6 Die .... Reihenhäuser sind schön. (*pl.*, neugebaut__)

7 Heute gehen wir in den .... Freizeitpark. (*m.*, modern__)

8 Wir müssen dieses .... Fahrrad sauber machen. (*n.*, schmutzig__)

9 Morgen gehen wir ins .... Einkaufszentrum. (*n.*, neu__)

10 Der .... Zug kommt um ein Uhr an. (*m.*, verspätet__)

Adjectives after the indefinite article have various endings. This also applies to **kein**, **mein**, **sein**, etc.

	m.	**f.**	**n.**	**pl.**
Nominative	ein klein**er** Hund	eine klein**e** Maus	ein klein**es** Haus	meine klein**en** Kinder
Accusative	einen klein**en** Hund	eine klein**e** Maus	ein klein**es** Haus	meine klein**en** Kinder
Dative	einem klein**en** Hund	einer klein**en** Maus	einem klein**en** Haus	meinen klein**en** Kinder**n**

B Fill the gaps with the suggested adjective and its correct ending.

1 München ist eine .... Stadt. (*f.*, umweltfreundlich__)

2 Ich suche ein .... T-Shirt. (*n.*, preiswert__)

3 Marta hat ihre .... Handtasche verloren. (*f.*, modisch__)

4 Wir haben unsere .... Hausaufgaben nicht gemacht. (*pl.*, schwierig__)

5 Ich habe ein .... Bett gekauft. (*n.*, bequem__)

6 Das ist ein .... Problem. (*n.*, groß__)

7 Das war vielleicht eine .... Stunde! (*f.*, langweilig__)

8 Diese .... Leute haben das Spiel verdorben. (*pl.*, idiotisch__)

9 Mein Vater hat einen .... Unfall gehabt. (*m.*, schwer__)

10 Klaus liebt seine .... Freundin. (*f.*, neu__)

11 Wir haben kein .... Obst. (*n.*, frisch__)

12 Maria hat einen .... Mantel gekauft. (*m.*, grün__)

Comparisons

> To make comparisons between things, you use the comparative or superlative.
>
> Add -**er** for the comparative, or add -**(e)ste** for the superlative.
>
> Adjective: langsam – langsamer – langsamst- + ending (*slow, slower, slowest*)
>
> Adverb: langsam – langsamer – am langsamsten (*slowly, more slowly, most slowly*)

A Insert the comparative and superlative forms.

1 Mathe ist langweilig, Physik ist ...., aber das .... Fach ist Kunst.

2 Oliver läuft schnell, Ali läuft ...., aber Tim läuft am ....

3 Berlin ist schön, Paris ist ...., aber Venedig ist die .... Stadt.

4 Madonna ist cool, Lady Gaga ist ...., aber Beyoncé ist die .... Sängerin.

5 Metallica ist .... als Guns N' Roses. (laut)

6 Bremen ist .... als Hamburg. (klein)

7 Deine Noten sind schlecht, aber meine sind noch ....

8 Ich finde Englisch .... als Französisch, aber Deutsch finde ich am .... (einfach)

9 Skifahren ist .... als Radfahren. (schwierig)

10 Mein Auto ist .... als dein Auto, aber das Auto meines Vaters ist am .... (billig)

> Some adjectives have small changes to the comparative and superlative forms.

B Fill in the gaps with the words provided below, then translate the sentences into English.

beste / länger / höher / besser / größer / jünger / am längsten

1 Ich bin .... als du. (jung)

2 Die Alpen sind .... als Snowdon. (hoch)

3 München ist .... als Bonn. (groß)

4 Meine Haare sind lang, Timos Haare sind ...., aber deine Haare sind ....

5 Fußball ist gut, Handball ist ...., aber Tennis ist das .... Spiel.

1 ....

2 ....

3 ....

4 ....

5 ....

C Compare your likes and dislikes by using *gern*, *lieber* and *am liebsten*.

1 Ich spiele .... Korbball. (*like*)

2 Ich esse .... Gemüse als Fleisch. (*prefer*)

3 Am .... gehe ich schwimmen. (*like best*)

Personal pronouns

Like *der*, *die* and *das*, pronouns change depending on what case they are in: nominative, accusative or dative.

Nominative	Accusative	Dative
ich	mich	mir
du	dich	dir
er	ihn	ihm
sie	sie	ihr
es	es	ihm
wir	uns	uns
ihr	euch	euch
Sie / sie	Sie / sie	Ihnen / ihnen

A Use the correct pronoun in the appropriate case.

1 Ich liebe .... (*you, familiar*)

2 Liebst du .... ? (*me*)

3 Kommst du mit .... ? (*me*)

4 Mein Bruder ist nett. Ich mag .... gern. (*him*)

5 Ich habe keine Kreditkarte. Ich habe .... verloren. (*it*)

6 Ein Geschenk für .... ? Danke! (*us*)

7 Wir haben .... gestern gesehen. (*you, plural, familiar*)

8 Haben .... gut geschlafen? (*you, formal*)

9 Die Party ist bei .... (*me*)

10 Rolf hatte Hunger. Ich bin mit .... essen gegangen. (*him*)

11 Vergiss .... nicht! (*me*)

12 Wie heißt .... ? (*you, familiar*)

13 Wie heißen .... ? (*you, formal*)

14 Meine Schwester ist krank. Gestern sind wir zu .... gegangen. (*her*)

15 Was ist los mit .... ? (*you, familiar*)

Certain special phrases use a dative pronoun.

es tut **mir** leid	*I am sorry*
es gefällt **ihm**	*he likes it*
es fällt **mir** schwer	*I find it difficult*
es geht **mir** gut	*I'm well*
es tut **ihr** weh	*it hurts her*
das schmeckt **mir**	*that tastes good*
das ist **mir** egal	*it's all the same to me*

B Fill in the gaps.

1 Schwimmen .... mir .... (= *I find it hard*)

2 Mmmm, Eis! .... es .... ? (= *do you [familiar] like the taste?/do you like it?*)

3 Aua! Das .... weh! (= *it hurts me*)

4 Leider .... es .... nicht gut. (= *we aren't well*)

5 Wer gewinnt im Fußball? Das .... (= *I don't care*)

6 Es .... leid. (= *we are sorry*)

Word order

> In German sentences, the **second** item is always the verb. In the perfect tense, the part of **haben** or **sein** comes in second position (see below).
>
> Daniel **fährt** in die Stadt.
> Morgen **fährt** Daniel in die Stadt.

A Rewrite these sentences with the new beginnings.

   1 Die Fernsehsendung beginnt.

   Um sechs Uhr ....

   2 Ich fahre mit dem Bus zur Arbeit.

   Jeden Tag ....

   3 Meine Eltern sind krank.

   Leider ....

   4 Man darf nicht rauchen.

   Hier ....

> In the perfect tense, the part of **haben** or **sein** comes in second position.
>
> Ich **bin** in den Jugendklub gegangen.
> Am Samstag **bin** ich in den Jugendklub gegangen.

B Now rewrite these sentences.

   1 Wir haben Eis gegessen.

   Gestern ....

   2 Timo ist ins Kino gegangen.

   Manchmal ....

   3 Ali ist nach Frankreich gefahren.

   Letztes Jahr ....

   4 Du hast Pommes gekauft.

   Heute Morgen ....

> Remember the word order in German: first **time**, then **manner**, then **place**.
>
>   T   M   P
> Ich spiele jeden Tag mit meinem Bruder im Garten.

C Write out these sentences in the right order.

   1 jeden Tag / Ich fahre / zur Schule / mit dem Rad

   ....

   2 am Wochenende / Gehst du / ins Schwimmbad? / mit mir

   ....

   3 oft / fern / Wir sehen / im Wohnzimmer

   ....

   4 Tischtennis / Mehmet spielt / im Jugendklub / abends

   ....

   5 im Büro / Mein Vater arbeitet / fleißig / seit 20 Jahren

   ....

   6 heute Abend / Willst du / Pizza essen? / im Restaurant / mit mir

   ....

Conjunctions

The most common conjunction that introduces a subordinate clause is **weil** (because). It sends the verb to the end.

Ich gehe oft auf Partys, **weil** sie lustig sind.

A Join these sentences together using **weil**. Write the sentences out.

1 Claudia will Sportlehrerin werden. Sie ist sportlich.

....

2 Ich kann dich nicht anrufen. Ich habe mein Handy verloren.

....

3 Wir fahren nach Spanien. Das Wetter ist dort so schön.

....

4 Du darfst nicht im Garten spielen. Es regnet.

....

5 Peter hat seine Hausaufgaben nicht gemacht. Er ist faul.

....

6 Ich mag Computerspiele. Sie sind so spannend.

....

The following conjunctions also send the verb to the end: **als**, **bevor**, **bis**, **da**, **damit**, **dass**, **nachdem**, **ob**, **obwohl**, **während**, **was**, **wie**, **wenn**. In the perfect tense, the part of **haben** or **sein** comes last. In the future tense, it is **werden** that comes at the end.

Ich habe Golf gespielt, **während** du eingekauft hast.

B Join the sentences together using the conjunction indicated. Write the sentences out.

1 Du kannst abwaschen. Ich koche. (während)

....

2 Wir kaufen oft ein. Wir sind in der Stadt. (wenn)

....

3 Ich kann nicht zur Party kommen. Ich werde arbeiten. (da)

....

4 Lasst uns früh aufstehen. Wir können wandern. (damit)

....

5 Meine Eltern waren böse. Ich bin nicht spät nach Hause gekommen. (obwohl)

....

6 Ich habe es nicht gewusst. Du bist krank. (dass)

....

7 Papa hat geraucht. Er war jung. (als)

....

8 Ich weiß nicht. Man repariert einen Computer. (wie)

....

9 Wir können schwimmen gehen. Das Wetter ist gut. (wenn)

....

10 Wir müssen warten. Es regnet nicht mehr. (bis)

....

More on word order

> **um … zu** means 'in order to'. It needs an infinitive at the end of the clause.
>
>   Wir gehen in den Park, **um** Tennis **zu** spielen.

A Combine these sentences with **um … zu**.

   1 Wir fahren in die Stadt. Wir kaufen Lebensmittel.

   ....

   2 Viele Leute spielen Tennis. Sie werden fit.

   ....

   3 Boris spart Geld. Er kauft ein Motorrad.

   ....

   4 Meine Schwester geht zur Abendschule. Sie lernt Französisch.

   ....

   5 Ich bin gestern zum Imbiss gegangen. Ich esse Pommes.

   ....

> There are some other expressions which use **zu** in the same way.

B Complete the sentences.

   1 Das Orchester beginnt .... (*to play*)

   2 Wir hoffen, ... (*to learn Spanish*)

   3 Oliver versucht, ... (*to play guitar*)

> Relative pronouns, **der**, **die** or **das** (expressing 'who' or 'that' or 'which'), send the verb to the end of the clause.
>
>   das Mädchen, das krank ist   *the girl who is ill*

C Translate these expressions into German. You will find the expressions jumbled up in the box below.

   1 the girl who plays tennis

   ....

   2 the boy who sings well

   ....

   3 the man who speaks German

   ....

   4 the house (*n.*) that is old

   ....

   5 the subject (*n.*) that is hard

   ....

   6 the car (*n.*) that is broken

   ....

   7 the cup (*f.*) that is full

   ....

das Auto,	das Fach,	der Deutsch spricht	das alt ist
der Junge,	das Mädchen,	das kaputt ist	das schwer ist
der Mann,	das Haus,	der gut singt	die voll ist
die Tasse,			das Tennis spielt

The present tense

> Verb endings in the present tense change according to who or what is doing the action.
>
> | ich | mach**e** | *I do / make* |
> | du | mach**st** | *you do / make* |
> | er / sie / es | mach**t** | *he / she / one does / makes* |
> | wir | mach**en** | *we do / make* |
> | ihr | mach**t** | *you do / make* |
> | Sie / sie | mach**en** | *they / you do / make* |

A Write in the correct form of the verb indicated. These verbs are all regular in the present tense.

1 wir .... (*go*)

2 er ...., ... (*find*)

3 sie .... (*sing*)

4 ich .... (*play*)

5 ihr .... (*do*)

6 du .... (*say*)

7 es .... (*come*)

8 sie (*plural*) .... (*swim*)

9 ich .... (*hear*)

10 wir .... (*drink*)

> Some verbs have a vowel change in the **du** and **er / sie / es** forms of the present tense. Choose from those provided below.

B Insert the correct form of the present tense, then translate the sentences into English.

schläfst / fahrt / esst / isst / gibt / spricht / sprecht / nimmst / liest / lest / fährt / hilfst

1 Was .... du? (lesen)

2 .... du? (schlafen)

3 Annabelle .... nicht gern Fleisch. (essen)

4 Kerstin .... gut Englisch. (sprechen)

5 .... du Zucker? (nehmen)

6 Ben .... bald nach Berlin. (fahren)

7 .... du mir bitte? (helfen)

8 Mein Onkel .... mir 20 Euro. (geben)

1 ....

2 ....

3 ....

4 ....

5 ....

6 ....

7 ....

8 ....

C Circle any irregular present tense verbs in this list.

er spricht / du siehst / sie macht / es liegt / ich sage / sie fährt / du kommst / er liest

More on verbs

> Separable verbs have two parts: a prefix and the main verb. In a sentence, the prefix goes to the end.
>
> einsteigen (*to get in*): Ich **steige** (*verb*) in das Taxi **ein** (*prefix*).

A Fill in the two gaps in these sentences.

1 Wir .... (abwaschen)

2 Er .... um 7 Uhr .... (aufwachen)

3 Wir .... oft Filme .... (herunterladen)

4 Wie oft .... du ....? (fernsehen)

5 Wo .... man ....? (aussteigen)

6 Ich .... nie .... (abwaschen)

> Separable verbs form the past participle as one word with the **ge-** in the middle: **ausgestiegen**.

B Put the above sentences into the perfect tense.

1 ....

2 ....

3 ....

4 ....

5 ....

6 ....

> Reflexive verbs are always used with a reflexive pronoun (**mich**, **dich**, **sich**, etc.).
>
> Ich wasche **mich** im Badezimmer.
>
> | ich freue **mich** | wir freuen **uns** |
> |---|---|
> | du freust **dich** | ihr freut **euch** |
> | er / sie / es freut **sich** | Sie / sie freuen **sich** |

C Fill in the correct reflexive pronoun, then translate the sentences into English.

1 Ich interessiere .... für Geschichte.

2 Sara freut .... auf die Ferien.

3 Erinnerst du .... an mich?

4 Wir langweilen .... in der Schule.

5 Ich habe .... noch nicht entschieden.

6 Dieter hat .... heute noch nicht rasiert.

7 Habt ihr .... gut amüsiert?

8 Unser Haus befindet .... in der Nähe vom Bahnhof.

1 ....

2 ....

3 ....

4 ....

5 ....

6 ....

7 ....

8 ....

Commands

When telling someone what to do using the *Sie* (polite) form, swap the present tense round so the verb comes before the pronoun.

  Stehen Sie auf!

A Tell someone …

   1 … not to park here. (parken)

   ....

   2 … not to talk so loudly. (sprechen)

   ....

   3 … to get off here. (aussteigen)

   ....

   4 … not to drive so fast. (fahren)

   ....

   5 … to come in. (hereinkommen)

   ....

   6 … to go straight on. (gehen)

   ....

   7 … to come back soon. (kommen)

   ....

   8 … to give you 10 euros. (geben)

   ....

When telling someone what to do using the *du* (familiar) form, use the present tense *du* form minus the -*st* ending.

  Steh auf!

B Tell a friend…

   1 … to get up. (aufstehen)

   ....

   2 … to write soon. (schreiben)

   ....

   3 … to come here. (herkommen)

   ....

   4 … to take two. (nehmen)

   ....

   5 … to bring you the ball. (bringen)

   ....

   6 … to stop. (aufhören)

   ....

   7 … to behave. (sich benehmen)

   ....

   8 … to sit down. (sich setzen)

   ....

Present tense modals

> Modal verbs (**können**, **müssen**, **wollen**, **dürfen**, **sollen**, **mögen**) can't be used on their own. They need to be used with the infinitive of another verb at the end of the sentence.

A Write in the modal verb and the infinitive. Use words from the box below.

1 Ich .... nicht schnell .... (*can't run*)

2 Wir .... bald Kaffee .... (*must buy*)

3 Kinder .... keinen Alkohol .... (*shouldn't drink*)

4 Claudia .... nicht .... (*doesn't like to swim*)

5 Schüler .... hier nicht .... (*aren't allowed to sit*)

6 Wir .... Pommes .... (*want to eat*)

7 Hier .... man .... (*is allowed to park*)

8 Meine Eltern .... eine neue Wohnung .... (*want to buy*)

9 Du .... gut Fußball .... (*can play*)

10 Sie (*polite*) .... höflich .... (*should be*)

> darf / dürfen / kann / kannst / müssen / sollten / sollten / mag / wollen /wollen
> essen / kaufen / kaufen / laufen / parken / sein / sitzen / spielen / trinken / schwimmen

B Make these sentences into modal sentences, using the verbs provided.

Man trinkt nicht zu viel. ⟶ Man **soll** nicht zu viel **trinken**.

1 Im Kino raucht man nicht. (dürfen)

....

2 Wir gehen zur Bowlingbahn. (können)

....

3 Meine Freunde bleiben zu Hause. (wollen)

....

4 Ihr esst weniger. (müssen)

....

5 Wir fahren nach München. (wollen)

....

6 Ergül spielt gut Gitarre. (können)

....

7 Hilfst du mir bei meinen Hausaufgaben? (können)

....

8 Man betritt den Rasen nicht. (dürfen)

....

9 Wir fahren mit der Straßenbahn. (müssen)

....

10 Ich esse meinen Salat nicht. (wollen)

....

Imperfect modals

To use modals in the past, take the imperfect of the modal verb and the infinitive is sent to the end of the sentence.

müssen	muss**te**	*had to*
wollen	woll**te**	*wanted to*
dürfen	dur**fte**	*was allowed to*
sollen	soll**te**	*was supposed to*
mögen	moch**te**	*liked*
können	konn**te**	*was able to / could*

A Put these present modals into the imperfect.

1 ich will ....

2 wir müssen ....

3 sie können ....

4 sie darf ....

5 man soll ....

6 er mag ....

7 wir wollen ....

8 Jutta kann ....

B Put these modal sentences into the imperfect.

Er kann gut singen. ⟶ Er **konnte** gut singen.

1 Du kannst mitspielen.

....

2 Wir müssen nach Hause gehen.

....

3 Ella mag nicht Musik hören.

....

4 Wir wollen im Internet surfen.

....

5 Ich kann gut Tischtennis spielen.

....

6 Ihr dürft spät ins Bett gehen.

....

Möchte (would like to) and *könnte* (could) are very useful forms. They also send the infinitive to the end.

C Translate these sentences.

May I sit here? ⟶ Darf ich hier sitzen?

1 Would you (*Sie*) like to play tennis?

....

2 We could go shopping.

....

3 I'd like to eat an ice cream.

....

4 Could you (*du*) help me?

....

The perfect tense 1

> Use the perfect tense to talk about something you have done in the past.
>
> Form the perfect tense by using the verb **haben** plus the past participle at the end of the sentence.
>
> Wir **haben** zu viel **gegessen**.

A Unjumble these perfect tense sentences.

1 Wir gespielt haben Minigolf.

....

2 gekauft ihr neue Habt Schuhe?

....

3 besucht du deine Hast Oma?

....

4 Was gesagt hat er?

....

5 habe Ich gelernt Spanisch.

....

6 Hast gelesen du Harry Potter?

....

7 ein Geschenk Dennis gegeben hat mir

....

8 gesehen einen haben tollen Wir Film.

....

> Some verbs of movement use **sein** instead of **haben** to form the perfect tense.

B Insert the correct form of **sein** and a past participle.

1 Wohin .... du .... ? (fahren)

2 Wir .... nach Mallorca .... (fahren).

3 Ich .... zu Hause .... (bleiben)

4 Usain Bolt .... schnell .... (laufen)

5 Meine Mutter .... nach Amerika .... (fliegen)

6 Der Zug .... (abfahren)

C Circle the correct verb: **haben** or **sein**.

1 Abdul hat / ist 12 Stunden geschlafen.

2 Wir haben / sind unsere Hausaufgaben gemacht.

3 Wohin hast / bist du gefahren?

4 Ich habe / bin spät nach Hause gekommen.

5 Habt / Seid ihr Britta gesehen?

The perfect tense 2

Many past participles are irregular and just have to be learnt.

A What are the past participles of these common verbs?

1 schwimmen ....
2 sein ....
3 schließen ....
4 essen ....
5 stehen ....
6 sitzen ....
7 schreiben ....
8 sterben ....

9 sprechen ....
10 treffen ....
11 werden ....
12 trinken ....
13 nehmen ....
14 singen ....
15 haben ....

B Now put these simple sentences into the perfect tense.

Wir sehen einen Film. ⟶ Wir **haben** einen Film **gesehen**.

1 Wir schreiben eine E-Mail.

....

2 Wir treffen uns um 6 Uhr.

....

3 Mein Onkel stirbt.

....

4 Nimmst du mein Handy?

....

5 Ich esse eine Bratwurst.

....

6 Er trinkt ein Glas Cola.

....

7 Wir schwimmen im Meer.

....

8 Marita spricht Italienisch.

....

(a) Separable verbs add the *ge* between the prefix and the verb.

einladen ⟶ ein**ge**laden

(b) Verbs starting **be**-, **emp**-, **er**- or **ver**- don't add *ge* to the past participle.

verstehen ⟶ verstanden

C Work out the past participles of these verbs.

1 vergessen ....
2 aufstehen ....
3 empfehlen ....
4 verlieren ....

5 besuchen ....
6 herunterladen ....
7 abfahren ....
8 aussteigen ....

The imperfect tense

> To form the imperfect (simple past) of regular verbs, take the **–en** off the infinitive, then add **t** and the ending.
>
> | | |
> |---|---|
> | ich hör**te** | *I heard / was hearing* |
> | du hör**test** | *you heard / were hearing* |
> | er / sie / man hör**te** | *he / she / one heard / was hearing* |
> | wir hör**ten** | *we heard / were hearing* |
> | ihr hör**tet** | *you heard / were hearing* |
> | Sie / sie hör**ten** | *you / they heard / were hearing* |

A Put these simple sentences into the imperfect.

    Wir hören Musik. ⟶ Wir **hörten** Musik.

1 Ich spiele am Computer.

....

2 Was sagst du?

....

3 Nina kauft Kaugummi.

....

4 Die Schüler lernen Englisch.

....

5 Es schneit im Winter.

....

6 Peter lacht laut.

....

> **Haben** and **sein** have an irregular imperfect form: **hatte** and **war**, plus the appropriate endings.

B Fill the gaps with the imperfect tense of **sein** or **haben**.

1 Es .... gestern kalt.

2 Wir .... auf der Party viel Spaß.

3 Paul .... im Krankenhaus.

4 Ihre Eltern .... drei Kinder.

5 Ich .... gestern im Imbiss.

6 .... du Angst?

> There are some irregular imperfect tense verbs which have to be learnt.

C Write **P** if the verb is in the present tense and **I** if it is in the imperfect.

1	Es gab viel zu essen.	....	**7**	Sie kamen um 6 Uhr an.	....
2	Wir sitzen im Kino.	....	**8**	Wie findest du das?	....
3	Es tut mir leid!	....	**9**	Aua! Das tat weh!	....
4	Ich fahre nach Berlin.	....	**10**	Ich fand es gut.	....
5	Er kommt früh an.	....	**11**	Es gibt nicht viel zu tun.	....
6	Er saß im Wohnzimmer.	....	**12**	Klaus fuhr zu schnell.	....

The future tense

It is quite normal to use the present tense to indicate the future.

  Ich komme bald nach Hause.   *I'm coming home soon.*

A Use the present tense to indicate the future. Put the future expression straight after the verb.

    Wir (gehen) einkaufen (morgen). ⟶ Wir gehen morgen einkaufen.

1 Susi (gehen) auf die Uni (nächstes Jahr).

....

2 Wir (fahren) nach Ibiza (im Sommer).

....

3 Er (kommen) zu uns (übermorgen).

....

4 Ich (bleiben) zu Hause (heute Abend).

....

5 (Bringen) du deine Schwester mit (am Wochenende)?

....

To form the actual future tense, use the present tense of **werden** with the infinitive at the end of the sentence.

ich werde	wir werden
du wirst	ihr werdet
er / sie / man wird	Sie / sie werden

B Insert the correct form of **werden** and the appropriate infinitive from the box below.

    Olaf **wird** Cola **trinken**.

1 Ich .... um 6 Uhr .... (*get up*)

2 .... du am Wochenende Musik .... ? (*listen*)

3 .... ihr Pizza .... ? (*eat*)

4 Wir .... die Prüfung .... (*pass*)

5 Nächstes Jahr .... wir nach Afrika .... (*travel*)

6 Daniel .... einen Film .... (*download*)

7 Ich .... ein Problem mit meinem Laptop .... (*have*)

8 Bayern München .... das Spiel .... (*win*)

9 Meine Freunde .... um 9 Uhr .... (*arrive*)

10 Meine Schwester .... im August .... (*get married*)

heiraten / fahren / hören / essen / herunterladen / gewinnen / haben / ankommen / aufstehen / bestehen

C Write three true sentences about things you will do in the future.

1 ....

....

2 ....

....

3 ....

....

The conditional

> To form the conditional, use part of **würde** plus the infinitive at the end.
>
> | | |
> |---|---|
> | ich würde | wir würden |
> | du würdest | ihr würdet |
> | er / sie / man würde | Sie / sie würden |

A Fill in the correct part of **würde**.

1 Wenn wir Zeit hätten, ... wir einkaufen gehen.

2 Wenn meine Eltern Geld hätten, ... sie ein Auto kaufen.

3 Wenn ich Kinder hätte, ... ich sie lieben.

4 Wenn Tanja nicht krank wäre, ... sie Skateboard fahren.

5 Wenn du fleißiger wärst, ... du deine Prüfung bestehen.

6 Wenn das Wetter besser wäre, ... wir Sport treiben.

> The conditional of **haben** is **hätte**, with the appropriate endings. The conditional of **sein** is **wäre**, with the appropriate endings.

B Put in the right form of **hätte** or **wäre**.

1 Wenn ich Krankenschwester .... , würde ich mich freuen.

2 Wenn er Klempner .... , würde er viel verdienen.

3 Wenn wir in einer Fabrik arbeiten würden, ... wir müde.

4 Wenn wir Glasflaschen .... , würden wir sie recyceln.

5 Wenn ich Hunger .... , würde ich eine Bratwurst essen.

6 Wenn Manya und Timo Talent .... , würden sie in einer Band spielen.

> | | |
> |---|---|
> | ich möchte | *I would like* |
> | ich hätte gern | *I would like to have* |

C Write three sentences about things you would like to do. Start with **Ich möchte ...**

1 ....

....

2 ....

....

3 ....

....

D Write three sentences about things you'd like to have. Start with **Ich hätte gern ...**

1 ....

....

2 ....

....

3 ....

....

The pluperfect tense

> To form the pluperfect (i.e. what *had* happened), use the imperfect form of **haben** or **sein** plus the past participle at the end.
>
> ich hatte (*I had, etc.*)   wir hatten
> du hattest   ihr hattet
> er / sie / man hatte   Sie / sie hatten
>
> Ich **hatte** mein Buch vergessen.   *I **had** forgotten my book.*

A Put in the right part of **haben** or **sein**, plus a past participle, to make these sentences pluperfect.

1 Wir .... Kaffee und Kuchen .... (*ordered*)

2 .... du Spaß .... ? (*had*)

3 Ich .... eine neue Stelle .... (*got*)

4 Wir .... unsere Freunde .... (*invited*)

5 Nachdem ich nach Hause .... (*came*), habe ich gegessen.

6 Ergül .... zur Bäckerei .... (*gone*)

7 Sie (*plural*) .... zu Hause .... (*stayed*)

8 Ich .... mit dem Auto nach Frankfurt .... (*driven*)

B Write out these perfect tense sentences in the pluperfect. You only need to change the part of **haben** or **sein**.

1 Es ist überhaupt nicht passiert.

   ....

2 Ich habe dir eine E-Mail geschickt.

   ....

3 Hast du dich nicht rasiert?

   ....

4 Ich bin sehr früh eingeschlafen.

   ....

5 Opa ist noch nie nach London gefahren.

   ....

6 Bist du zur Haltestelle gegangen?

   ....

7 Wir haben unseren Müll zur Mülldeponie gebracht.

   ....

8 Er hat zwei Computerspiele heruntergeladen.

   ....

9 Die Fabrik ist geschlossen worden.

   ....

10 Fatima hat Abitur gemacht.

   ....

Questions

> To ask a simple question, just turn the pronoun (or name) and the verb around.
>
>   Du bist krank. ⟶ Bist du krank?

A Make these statements into questions.

1 Kevin spielt oft am Computer.

....

2 Du hast dein Handy verloren.

....

3 Wir wollen Volleyball spielen.

....

4 Hakan studiert Informatik.

....

5 Ihr geht morgen zum Sportzentrum.

....

B Ask the questions to which these are the answers.

  Ja, ich habe Chips gekauft. ⟶ Hast du Chips gekauft?

1 Nein, ich bin nicht zum Supermarkt gefahren.

....

2 Ja, Ayse wird Chemie studieren.

....

3 Nein, mein Auto ist nicht kaputt.

....

4 Ja, ich esse gern Bratwurst mit Pommes.

....

5 Ich weiß nicht, ob es morgen regnen wird.

....

> You have to learn the German question words.

C Draw lines to link the English and German question words.

who?	wessen?
what?	wie viele?
how?	warum?
when?	was für?
why?	wer?
where?	mit wem?
how many?	wie?
what kind of?	wann?
whose?	was?
who with?	wo?

D Write three questions you could ask using the question words above.

1 ....

2 ....

3 ....

Time markers

> Time markers are useful words for showing when something happens, did happen or will happen.

A Write what tense (present, past or future) these time markers indicate.

1	gestern	....	**6**	normalerweise	....
2	früher	....	**7**	vor zwei Wochen	....
3	bald	....	**8**	morgen	....
4	letzte Woche	....	**9**	nächste Woche	....
5	heute	....	**10**	jetzt	....

B Draw lines to link the English and German expressions.

manchmal	*immediately*
neulich	*on time*
sofort	*sometimes*
täglich	*in the future*
rechtzeitig	*recently*
in Zukunft	*every day*

C Rewrite these sentences using the time expressions provided. Put the time expression first and the verb second.

Wir fahren nach Bremen. (morgen) ⟶ Morgen fahren wir nach Bremen.

1 Ich werde mein Betriebspraktikum machen. (nächste Woche)

....

....

2 Ulli sieht fern. (heute Abend)

....

....

3 Man wird Strom sparen. (in Zukunft)

....

....

4 Du wirst einen Unfall haben. (bald)

....

....

5 Wir treffen uns mit unseren Freunden. (manchmal)

....

....

6 Ich war bei meinem Onkel. (neulich)

....

....

7 Mehmet hat sein Betriebspraktikum begonnen. (vorgestern)

....

....

8 Ich gehe zur Bäckerei. (jeden Tag)

....

....

Numbers

Revise the numbers 1–1000. You need to be completely confident in using numbers.

A Write the German numbers in figures.

1 vierhunderteinundzwanzig ....

2 tausendsechshundertvierundvierzig ....

3 achtundsechzig ....

4 dreihunderteins ....

5 siebenundneunzig ....

6 hundertfünf ....

7 siebzehn ....

8 sechshundertdreiundfünfzig ....

B Write in the German numbers. Choose from the box below.

1 Es ist .... nach .... (20, 9)

2 Ausverkauf! .... Prozent Rabatt! (15)

3 Es ist .... Grad. (13)

4 Ich habe .... Euro gewonnen. (650)

5 Der Zug kommt um .... Minuten vor .... an. (12, 7)

6 Es gibt .... Schüler in meiner Klasse. (30)

sieben / zwölf / dreißig / fünfzehn / dreizehn / sechshundertfünfzig / neun / zwanzig

Revise the ordinal numbers.

1st	erste	20th	zwanzigste
2nd	zweite	21st	einundzwanzigste
3rd	dritte	30th	dreißigste
4th	vierte	31st	einunddreißigste
5th	fünfte		
6th	sechste		
7th	siebte		

C Write the dates in numbers.

der einunddreißigste Mai ⟶ 31.5.

1 der zwölfte März ....

2 der dreizehnte Juli ....

3 der achtundzwanzigste Dezember ....

4 der erste April ....

5 der dritte Januar ....

6 der siebzehnte Juni ....

D Write in the ordinal numbers.

1 Mein Geburtstag ist am .... November. (*1st*)

2 Saschas Geburtstag ist am .... September. (*7th*)

3 Das Konzert findet am .... Mai statt. (*12th*)

4 Die Ferien beginnen am .... Juli. (*2nd*)

Practice Exam Paper: Reading

This Practice Exam Paper has been written to help you practise what you have learned and may not be representative of a real exam paper.

G Shopping

1 Look at the shopping list.

Which items from the list above have been bought?
Write the correct letter in the box.

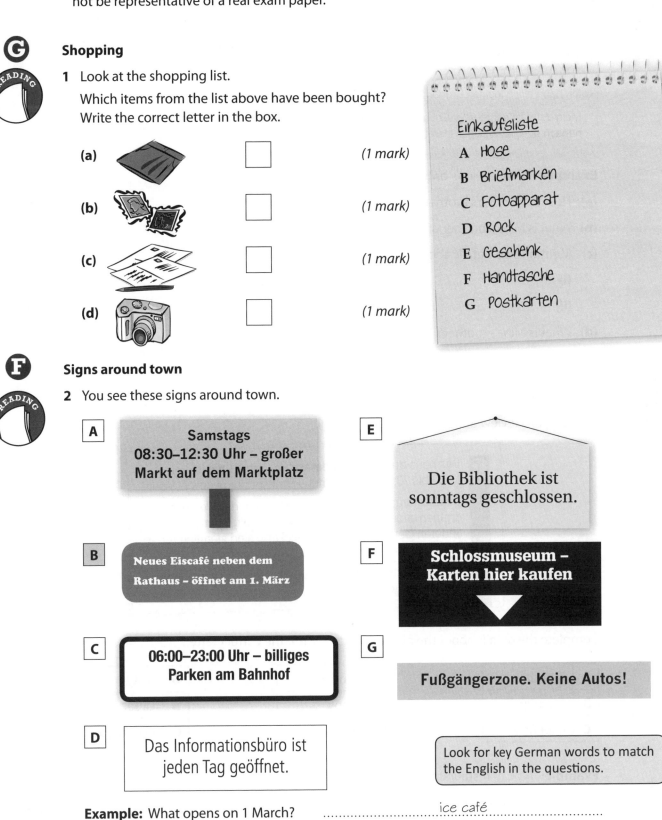

(a) [ ] *(1 mark)*

(b) [ ] *(1 mark)*

(c) [ ] *(1 mark)*

(d) [ ] *(1 mark)*

Einkaufsliste

A Hose
B Briefmarken
C Fotoapparat
D Rock
E Geschenk
F Handtasche
G Postkarten

F Signs around town

2 You see these signs around town.

A
**Samstags
08:30–12:30 Uhr – großer
Markt auf dem Marktplatz**

E
Die Bibliothek ist
sonntags geschlossen.

B
**Neues Eiscafé neben dem
Rathaus – öffnet am 1. März**

F
**Schlossmuseum –
Karten hier kaufen**

C
**06:00–23:00 Uhr – billiges
Parken am Bahnhof**

G
Fußgängerzone. Keine Autos!

D
Das Informationsbüro ist
jeden Tag geöffnet.

Look for key German words to match
the English in the questions.

Example: What opens on 1 March? .... *ice café* ....

(a) Where can you park cheaply? .... *(1 mark)*

(b) Where are cars not allowed? .... *(1 mark)*

(c) Which building is open every day? .... *(1 mark)*

(d) Which place is closed on Sundays? .... *(1 mark)*

My family

3 Read Mina's email.

> Löschen Antworten Antworten Alle Weiter Drucken
>
> Ich habe einen kleinen Bruder. Er heißt Tom und er ist fünf Jahre alt. Er ist oft sehr laut!
>
> Mein Vater ist sehr lustig. Er hat braune Haare und grüne Augen. Meine Mutter ist hübsch und hat lockige Haare. Sie ist wirklich nett.

Example: What is Mina's brother called? .... Tom ....

(a) How old is Mina's brother? .... *(1 mark)*

(b) What is Mina's brother often like? .... *(1 mark)*

(c) Mention **two** details about Mina's father.

    (i) .... *(1 mark)*

    (ii) .... *(1 mark)*

(d) What is Mina's mother's hair like? .... *(1 mark)*

A restaurant review

4 You read this review about a new restaurant.

> Das neue griechische **Restaurant am Fluss** ist von 12:00 bis 23:30 Uhr geöffnet. Es ist sonntags geschlossen.
>
> Das Restaurant ist klein, aber man kann draußen oder drinnen sitzen. Das Tagesgericht ist billig, aber die anderen Gerichte auf der Speisekarte sind ziemlich teuer. Das Schweinekotelett schmeckt wirklich gut.
>
> Man muss ziemlich lange warten, aber die Kellner sind sehr freundlich.

Complete the details about the new restaurant. Write the correct letter.

A	Monday		D	Sunday		G	tasty
B	friendly		E	funny		H	Greek
C	expensive		F	cheap		I	not so good

Example: Type of restaurant   H

(a) The restaurant is closed on   ☐.   *(1 mark)*

(b) The dish of the day is   ☐.   *(1 mark)*

> Don't just go for the first word you recognise. Look carefully at the choices.

(c) The pork is   ☐.   *(1 mark)*

(d) The waiters are   ☐.   *(1 mark)*

Part-time jobs

5 You read this article.

> Richard hat schon ein paar Nebenjobs gehabt.
>
> Seit Januar arbeitet er am Wochenende in einem Freizeitzentrum und das macht ihm viel Spaß. Als er jünger war, hat er jeden Tag Zeitungen ausgetragen, aber er hat nicht viel verdient.
>
> In den Sommerferien wird Richard als Kellner in einem Café in der Stadtmitte arbeiten. Er ist sehr froh, weil der Job gut bezahlt wird. Er hilft gern im Schnellimbiss im Freizeitzentrum, aber er braucht mehr Geld.
>
> Er hat auch drei Monate in einer Bäckerei gearbeitet, aber es gefiel ihm nicht, weil der Chef zu streng war.

Which **four** statements are correct?

A	Richard has had more than one part-time job.	**F**	Richard is looking forward to working as a waiter.
B	Richard has been working in the sports centre since January.	**G**	Richard has never worked in a snack bar before.
C	Richard used to deliver newspapers when he was younger.	**H**	Richard enjoyed working in a bakery.
D	Delivering newspapers was well paid.	**I**	The boss at the bakery was not very nice.
E	Richard is hoping to work in a café next year.		

Write the **four** correct letters in the boxes.

Example: | A | | | | |

(4 marks)

In a youth club

6 You read these comments.

> **Sophie:** Es gibt viel zu tun. Manchmal sehen wir Filme und das macht viel Spaß.
>
> **Esma:** Ich liebe Musik. Im Klub lerne ich, Klavier zu spielen. Am Freitag spielen wir in einem Konzert.
>
> **Hanna:** Im Moment machen wir einen kurzen Dokumentarfilm über den Klub und das ist wirklich interessant.
>
> **Adam:** Am See können wir angeln und ich finde das viel besser als Schwimmen.
>
> **Mehmet:** Ich kann mit anderen Jungen und Mädchen plaudern oder Musik hören.
>
> **Ben:** Manchmal kochen und essen wir gemeinsam. Letzte Woche habe ich mit drei Freunden Nudeln gekocht.
>
> **Iris:** Ich komme gern hierher, weil ich mich nie langweile. Das Computerzimmer ist wunderbar.

Write the initial of the person: **S** (Sophie), **E** (Esma), etc.

Who …

(a) plays a musical instrument? ☐ *(1 mark)* **(c)** chats to other young people? ☐ *(1 mark)*

(b) makes a meal? ☐ *(1 mark)* **(d)** makes a film? ☐ *(1 mark)*

B Hotel

7 Read the hotel review.

> Kinder und ihre Eltern sind bei uns willkommen und im Erdgeschoss gibt es einen Spielraum mit Fernsehapparat und einer guten Auswahl an Spielzeugen. Ein Babysittingdienst ist auch vorhanden.
>
> Alle Zimmer im ersten Stock haben eine herrliche Aussicht auf den See, wo man verschiedene Wassersportarten machen kann. Es gibt auch Tennisplätze in der Nähe und wir reservieren gern einen Platz für Sie.
>
> In der Nähe gibt es interessante Museen und Galerien sowie historische Sehenswürdigkeiten. Das alte Schloss ist besonders schön, aber nur im Sommer geöffnet. Mit der S-Bahn ist es nicht weit in die Stadtmitte, wo es tolle Klubs und Cafés für Jugendliche gibt.

Read the following sentences. Write **T** (True), **F** (False) or **?** (Not in the text) in the box.

(a) You can reach the hotel by public transport. ☐ *(1 mark)*

(b) The hotel has a library for guests. ☐ *(1 mark)*

(c) The first floor rooms are more expensive. ☐ *(1 mark)*

(d) All rooms have internet access. ☐ *(1 mark)*

(e) Children's facilities are in the basement. ☐ *(1 mark)*

(f) The hotel has a good view of the sea. ☐ *(1 mark)*

(g) You should book in advance to go to the castle. ☐ *(1 mark)*

(h) The town centre is not far away by suburban train. ☐ *(1 mark)*

A visit to an English school

B

8 Complete each of the following texts with one of the words which follow.

Write the correct letter in the box.

(a) Vor drei Wochen sind zwanzig Schüler aus Bonn nach England gefahren, weil sie ihre englischen Sprachkenntnisse ☐ wollten.

A	verbessern
B	vergessen
C	vermeiden

☐ *(1 mark)*

(b) Jeder Schüler muss jetzt über seine Erfahrungen an der englischen Schule schreiben. Sie haben eine Gesamtschule besucht und waren besonders froh, dass der Schultag ☐ angefangen hat. Eine halbe Stunde länger im Bett ist immer gut!

A	früher
B	um acht Uhr
C	später

☐ *(1 mark)*

(c) Die Schüler fanden die Unterschiede zwischen den Schulsystemen erstaunlich. Besonders gut fanden sie, dass man in England nicht ☐ muss, d.h. man bleibt mit den gleichen Klassenkameraden.

A	schwänzen
B	sitzen bleiben
C	Sport treiben

☐ *(1 mark)*

(d) Sie waren ein bisschen nervös, als sie in der Deutschstunde über ihr eigenes Schulsystem sprechen mussten, aber die englischen Schüler haben gerne zugehört, weil sie das Thema ☐ fanden.

A	langweilig
B	interessant
C	furchtbar

☐ *(1 mark)*

Sport

9 You read Hanna's blog.

> Ich bin ein großer Sportfan! Ich sehe gern Sport im Fernsehen. Manchmal gehe ich am Samstag mit meinem Vater ins Fußballstadion, und das finde ich noch besser, weil die Zuschauer immer so freundlich sind und mein Vater mir an der Wurstbude eine Wurst mit Pommes kauft.
>
> Als ich letzten April meine Freundin in London besucht habe, hatten wir Karten für ein Rugbyspiel im Stadion in Twickenham. Das Spiel war sehr spannend, aber ich fand die Regeln ziemlich kompliziert und es gab keinen Kommentator, der einem das alles erklären könnte. Leichtathletik ist viel einfacher!
>
> Seit sechs Jahren ist Leichtathletik ohne Zweifel die Sportart Nummer eins für mich. Ich mache Leichtathletik, weil ich fit bleiben will und weil es mir Spaß macht. Am Anfang habe ich zweimal pro Woche trainiert, aber jetzt trainiere ich viel öfter. Dienstags und donnerstags stehe ich früh auf, um vor der Schule joggen zu gehen. Samstags und sonntags trainiere ich im Stadion. Das ist anstrengend, aber es ist wichtig, weil ich meinen Platz im Verein nicht verlieren will.
>
> Um mich zu entspannen, gehe ich mindestens einmal pro Woche mit Freunden schwimmen. Mein Vater holt mich danach ab, aber er schwimmt nicht. Im Sommer fahren wir in ein Freibad in der Nachbarstadt.

(a) What is a positive and negative aspect of watching live sport, according to Hanna?

   (i) Positive: .... *(1 mark)*

   (ii) Negative: .... *(1 mark)*

(b) What exactly is Hanna's opinion of athletics?

.... *(1 mark)*

(c) How has Hanna's training schedule changed?

.... *(1 mark)*

(d) What motivates Hanna to train hard?

.... *(1 mark)*

(e) Why does Hanna go swimming?

.... *(1 mark)*

> Use any words which look like English words to help you get the gist of the text, before you do a detailed read.

Practice Exam Paper: Listening

This Practice Exam Paper has been written to help you practise what you have learned and may not be representative of a real exam paper.

 G

Clothes

1 Listen to what these people say they are wearing. Write the correct letter in the box.

Example:

A	B	C

A

(a)

A
B
C

☐ *(1 mark)*

(c)

A
B
C

☐ *(1 mark)*

(b)

A
B
C

☐ *(1 mark)*

(d)

A
B
C

☐ *(1 mark)*

 F

At school

2 Petra is talking about school.

Example: How does she get to school? .... *Bike* ....

(a) Which subject does she like? .... *(1 mark)*

(b) What is her favourite day? .... *(1 mark)*

(c) When does school finish? .... *(1 mark)*

(d) What does she do after school? .... *(1 mark)*

At the market

3 Olga is at the market. Which fruit and vegetables does she buy?

Write the **four** correct letters in the boxes.

Example: C

☐ ☐ ☐ ☐

(4 marks)

Directions

4 Leona is asking for directions.

A	in front of the department store
B	15 minutes
C	on the right
D	4.30
E	cathedral
F	5.30
G	straight on
H	in front of the town hall
I	30 minutes

Example: Leona wants to go to the E .

(a) The tram stop is ☐ and ☐ .

(2 marks)

(b) The trams run every ☐ .

(1 mark)

(c) The next one is due at ☐ .

(1 mark)

D **Herr Schreiber's breakfast**

5 Herr Schreiber is asking about breakfast at the hotel.

(a) What drink is offered for adults? .... *(1 mark)*

(b) Name one item of food available. .... *(1 mark)*

(c) What is the cost of breakfast in euros per person? .... *(1 mark)*

(d) What time does breakfast start? .... *(1 mark)*

> Make sure you are familiar with your numbers and times
> before the exam – they are bound to come up somewhere.

C **At the doctor's**

6 Why are these people visiting the doctor?

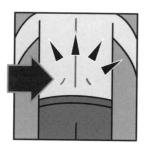

A

B

C

D

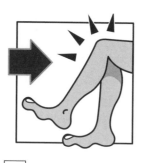

E

F

G

H

Write the correct letter in the box.

Example: H

(a) [ ] *(1 mark)* **(b)** [ ] *(1 mark)* **(c)** [ ] *(1 mark)* **(d)** [ ] *(1 mark)*

A guest house booking

7 The Deinhardt family are going to Germany. Mrs Deinhardt telephones the bed and breakfast to confirm her booking.

Write the correct letter in the box.

Example: The booking is for …

A	next week
B	tomorrow
C	next month

A

(a) Mrs Deinhardt is ringing because …

A	she wants to book a single room
B	there will be one person fewer in her group
C	she wants to change the date of arrival

(1 mark)

(b) Mrs Deinhardt's rooms…

A	have a balcony
B	look on to the river
C	look out on to a wood

(1 mark)

(c) The Deinhardt family will be arriving …

A	early morning
B	late at night
C	around midday

(1 mark)

(d) The family …

A	has never visited the area before
B	visited the area last year
C	normally comes to this area

(1 mark)

B   **Last weekend**

8 Listen to Felix describing his weekend.

What did he think of it?

Write **P** for positive.

Write **N** for negative.

Write **P + N** for positive and negative.

(a) [   ]   Listen for negatives.   *(1 mark)*

(b) [   ]   *(1 mark)*

(c) [   ]   *(1 mark)*

(d) [   ]   *(1 mark)*

A   **My best friend**

9 Some people are talking about their best friends. Write the correct letter in the box.

(a) What does Rene say about Pia?

A	We have been friends for years.
B	We get on well as we have a lot in common.
C	It took us some time to become friends.

[   ]   *(1 mark)*

(b) What does Ross say about Knut?

A	We have been friends since we were young.
B	Knut is often bad tempered.
C	Knut makes life fun.

[   ]   *(1 mark)*

(c) What does Ruth say about Karola?

A	Karola has good and bad characteristics.
B	Karola can be a bit selfish.
C	Karola never annoys me.

[   ]   *(1 mark)*

(d) What does Sebastian say about Adnan?

A	Adnan gets on well with my brother.
B	Adnan and I will be together next year.
C	Adnan and I are inseparable.

[   ]   *(1 mark)*

Zell am See

10 Listen to the tourist office manager, Frau Juric, talking about Zell am See.

(a) What has Zell am See been famous for since 1928?

.... *(1 mark)*

(b) Name two key features awaiting winter guests.

(i) .... *(1 mark)*

(ii) .... *(1 mark)*

(c) Who in particular might like to visit Zell am See in the summer?

.... *(1 mark)*

Shopping

11 Three people are talking about shopping. What are their opinions?

A Big shopping centres are great.

B People don't realise how damaging internet shopping is.

C People should always shop locally.

D Local shops should offer more services.

E Internet shopping is a good thing.

Write the correct letter in the box.

(a) Stephanie ☐ *(1 mark)*

(b) Jozo ☐ *(1 mark)*

(c) Ina ☐ *(1 mark)*

Answers

Lifestyle

1. Birthdays

1 **(a)** D **(b)** M **(c)** J **(d)** F

2 **(a)** (sometimes quite) expensive / loud
   (b) (pretty) flowers
   (c) January
   (d) (*any two of*) went to cinema / with three friends / had a sleepover / friends stayed the night
   (e) too loud

2. Pets

3 E, G, H, I

4 **(a)** A **(b)** C **(c)** C **(d)** B

3. Physical description

5 **(a)** H **(b)** F **(c)** D **(d)** I

6 **(a)** C **(b)** A **(c)** B **(d)** C
   (e) A

7 H, D, I, A, E

4. Character description

8 **(a)** A **(b)** C

9 **(a)** I **(b)** H **(c)** B **(d)** F

5. Brothers and sisters

10 **(a)** C **(b)** A **(c)** C **(d)** A

6. Family

11 **(a)** F **(b)** T **(c)** ? **(d)** F **(e)** F
   (f) ? **(g)** F **(h)** T **(i)** ?

7. Friends

12 **(a)** M **(b)** A **(c)** H **(d)** L

13 **(a) (i)** never answered a question / quiet in lessons / Melissa never noticed him
   (ii) she likes him now / finds him funny and happier
   (b) (i) (*any two of*) talked in class all the time / only did homework now and again / rude in class / kept in every week / sent to head
   (ii) new friends / nicer group of friends

8. Daily routine

14 Alex – F 6
   David – B 2
   Claudia – C 1
   Gabi – E 4

15 **(a) (i)** too many hours spent in classroom each day
   (ii) find school day OK / not tiring

(iii) stay in bed later / don't need to get up so early
(iv) school day to start at 9.30
(b) (i) give up break
(ii) uncertain it will make any difference

9. Breakfast

16 Kai – C 5
   Amir – G 3
   Angela – D 2
   Olivia – A 4

10. Eating at home

17 **(a)** C **(b)** B **(c)** A **(d)** B

18 **(a)** A, C **(b)** B, C

11. Eating in café

19 C, F, G, I

20 **(a)** C **(b)** H **(c)** D **(d)** B
   (e) F **(f)** I

12. Eating in a restaurant

21 **(a)** F **(b)** ? **(c)** F **(d)** T
   (e) ? **(f)** T **(g)** F **(h)** T **(i)** ?

22 **(a)** Most important: a very good selection on the menu (so you can go back and eat there again)
   (b) Negative **(i)** and **(ii)**: (*any two of*) main course was cold / unappetizing when it arrived / fork was dirty / service and food are bad

13. Healthy eating

23 **(a)** B + M **(b)** M **(c)** B **(d)** B
   (e) B + M **(f)** M

24 **(a) (i)** young people who are out and about and in a hurry / don't have time
   (ii) they grab unhealthy food
   (b) the food is bad for your heart
   (c) vegetarian diet + fish
   (d) bread but not white bread
   (e) don't eat it every day

14. Health issues

25 **(a)** E **(b)** M **(c)** T **(d)** F

26 **(a)** B **(b)** E **(c)** A

15. Health problems

27 C, G, B, H

28 **(a)** he doesn't enjoy it
   (b) the flat stinks of cigarettes
   (c) the air is fresher
   (d) (strong) coffee
   (e) sporty / never smoked

16. Future relationship plans

29 (a) A   (b) L   (c) A   (d) X
   (e) L   (f) X

30 (a) F   (b) C   (c) E   (d) A

17. Social issues

31 (a) his friend becoming homeless
   (b) want to help get people out of poverty
   (c) people to chat to / companionship / can discuss problems
   (d) nurse to talk to about worries / give advice
   (e) have to get there on the bus / on the edge of town / you can only stay one night

32 (a) B, C   (b) C, D

18. Social problems

33 (a) C   (b) A   (c) A   (d) C
34 B, D, F

Leisure

19. General hobbies

1 (a) B   (b) A   (c) C   (d) A
2 (a) texting
   (b) shopping
   (c) playing football
   (d) reading

20. Sport

3 Christine – A
   Gabi – B
   Ivor – G
   Anna – C
   Paul – I
   Kai – H

4 (a) B   (b) E   (c) C

21. Arranging to go out

5 (a) D   (b) C   (c) A   (d) B
   (e) C   (f) E   (g) A
6 (a) B   (b) B   (c) A   (d) C

22. What I did last weekend

7 (a) T   (b) T   (c) ?   (d) F   (e) T
   (f) ?   (g) T   (h) F
8 (a) P   (b) N   (c) N   (d) P + N

23. TV programmes

9 D, B, I, C
10 (a) P + N   (b) N   (c) P   (d) P

24. Cinema

11 (a) B   (b) A   (c) B   (d) C
12 (a) C   (b) C   (c) B

25. Music

13 B, C, G, I
14 (a) F   (b) A   (c) E

26. New technology

15 (a) his parents are unable to help him
   (b) they don't understand the internet
   (c) it can be dangerous
   (d) see what's on / read recommendations
   (e) her online purchase was never delivered and the money disappeared from her bank account

16 (a) downloading music
   (b) uploading photos
   (c) playing games with friends
   (d) reading the news

27. Language of the internet

17 (a) A   (b) G   (c) B   (d) F
18 (a) (i) (*either one*) visit clients / go to meetings
      (ii) (*either one*) it annoys her / she would rather work from home
      (iii) (*either one*) being correctly dressed / not to appear in her pyjamas for a video call
   (b) (i) her boss does not understand new technology
      (ii) (*one of*) saves time / money / energy if you work from home
      (iii) look for a new job at an internet firm

28. Internet pros and cons

19 (a) L   (b) A   (c) T   (d) O
20 (a) (i) homework
      (ii) goes to library
      (iii) remembering passwords
   (b) (i) same one for each site
      (ii) not a good idea
      (iii) ID theft
   (c) (i) business (trips)
      (iii) yesterday for her birthday

29. Shops

21 (a) €25.00   (b) €2.50   (c) €13.00
   (d) €5.60

22 (a) (i) shopping centre / town centre
      (ii) all under one roof
      (iii) buy CDs / DVDs for her family in the summer sale
      (iv) full of loud people
   (b) (i) they all have the same products / clothes
      (ii) they have more interesting clothes
      (iii) he buys fewer items / doesn't think you need hundreds of clothes in your wardrobe

(iv) if everyone bought from department / big stores and looked the same

30. Food shopping

23 B, D, G, H

24 **(a)** B **(b)** A **(c)** C **(d)** A

31. Shopping

25 **(a)** F **(b)** F **(c)** T **(d)** T
(e) ? **(f)** F **(g)** T
(h) ?

26 **(a)** his parents thought his old shoes too dirty for a job interview
(b) had nice and good value shoes in shop windows but they didn't fit
(c) good selection / shoe department full of children looking for (the latest) Disney trainers
(d) he found some shoes which were reduced and he had 10 euros cash left

32. Clothes and colours

27 Julia – F
Davran – H
Mario – B
Celina – A
Charline – I
Birk – C

28 **(a)** E, G **(b)** A, B

33. Buying clothes

29 **(a)** B **(b)** C **(c)** A **(d)** A

30 **(a)** P + N **(b)** N **(c)** P + N **(d)** P

34. Returning clothes

31 **(a)** J **(b)** A **(c)** E **(d)** F
(e) J **(f)** A

32 **(a)** B **(b)** C **(c)** A **(d)** C

35. Shopping opinions

33 **(a)** shopping has become a hobby / more popular than jogging / swimming
(b) **(i)** friends help him decide
(ii) friends don't pay
(c) (*any one*) she is not interested in it / can't stand it / prefers to do sport
(d) loves it
(e) **(i)** (*any one*) find items which are not too expensive / which are different / clothes particularly fashionable
(ii) not much choice

34 **(a)** N **(b)** P + N **(c)** P **(d)** N

36. Pocket money

35 **(a)** €2 **(b)** €30 **(c)** €17
(d) €300

36 **(a)** doesn't get money if he doesn't behave
(b) likes to save her money
(c) works to get his money so doesn't waste it

37. Holiday destinations

37 **(a)** L **(b)** A **(c)** B **(d)** A

38 **(a)** D **(b)** C **(c)** E **(d)** F

38. Holiday accommodation

39 **(a)** F **(b)** H **(c)** F **(d)** Y
(e) H **(f)** Y

40 **(a)** P + N **(b)** P **(c)** N

39. Booking accommodation

41 C, F, D, H

42 A, C, D, G

40. Staying in a hotel

43 **(a)** F **(b)** T **(c)** F **(d)** ?
(e) F C **(f)** ? **(g)** F **(h)** T

44 **(a)** a weekend
(b) in Spring
(c) a view of the lake
(d) the fifth floor / the wedding room / a room as big as a flat
(e) the bathroom / the huge bathtub / the sauna

41. Staying on a campsite

45 C, F, H, I

46 **(a)** C **(b)** A **(c)** A **(d)** B

42. Holiday activities

47 **(a)** need to relax after the long school year
(b) warmer weather
(c) their parents are not there
(d) (*either one*) take photos / sleep on bus
(e) police getting stricter: no alcohol on the beach and need shoes / T-shirts to go into bars
(f) she is not convinced it will have an effect on people's behaviour

48 A, C, D

43. Holiday preferences

49 Bernadette – E 4
Tom – A 6
Lea – F 1

50 **(a)** A, H **(b)** D, G

44. Holiday plans

51 C, E, G, H

52 **(a)** **(i)** there's a lot to see / excellent shopping
(ii) because her cousin stayed with Linda last year

(iii) she wants to study there later so wants to make sure she likes it
(b) (i) show her the sights
(ii) she is going snowboarding for the first time and it should be exciting

45. Past holidays

53 **(a)** C **(b)** C **(c)** B **(d)** A
(e) C **(f)** A **(g)** B **(h)** B

Home and entertainment

46. Countries

1 **(a)** L **(b)** S **(c)** A **(d)** M
2 **(a)** D **(b)** C **(c)** A

47. My house

3 B, E, F, H
4 **(a)** P **(b)** P **(c)** P + N **(d)** N

48. My room

5 D, C, G, E
6 **(a)** C **(b)** C **(c)** A **(d)** B

49. Helping at home

7 **(a)** B, C **(b)** D, E
8 **(a) (i)** has to stay at home to tidy her room
(ii) she wants to help her mum
(b) (i) has to stay at home to clean the windows
(ii) (*one of*) annoyed by his dad / doesn't know why he has to clean windows today / would prefer to go ice skating

50. Where I live

9 A, D, F, G
10 **(a) (i)** Positive: (*one of*) lively place / always something to do for children / adults / excellent / good value public transport / no need to go by car
(ii) Negative: no meadow / park near to apartment block
(b) (i) Positive: big house with a view of the wood
(ii) Negative: (*one of*) had to buy a second car / can't do anything without a car

51. Places in town

11 Markus – A
Viktoria – E
Johann – C
Marta – I
Paul – H
Stefanie – D
12 **(a)** shopping centre
(b) library

(c) shop
(d) monument

52. What to do in town

13 **(a)** (*either one*) many come each year / many return often
(b) A
(c) if you buy a special ticket you can travel more cheaply on public transport
(d) (*either one*) all kinds of interesting shops where you can buy souvenirs and gifts / enjoy specialities in the bars and restaurants
(e) most museums are closed on Mondays

53. Tourist attractions

14 **(a)** A **(b)** G **(c)** D **(d)** F
15 **(a)** B **(b)** C **(c)** C **(d)** A

54. Signs in town

16 **(a)** C **(b)** E **(c)** F **(d)** G
17 **(a)** tired
(b) she urgently needed a toilet
(c) thirsty
(d) C

55. Pros and cons of your town

18 Felix – H, B
Lilli – G
Sophie – A
19 **Milos**
(a) in the Black Forest / in south-west Germany
(b) excellent public transport / good value / fast public transport
(c) (*any two of*) can get a summer job / don't need a car / travel around easily by bike / one of the most environmentally friendly cities in Germany
(d) hire a car
Leonie
(a) not enough for young people to do
(b) can't move for tourists in the historical old town
(c) in a bigger town with more night clubs / cafes for young people
(d) her parents like the surrounding landscape and the parks in the town / would never move

56. Town description

20 **(a)** living abroad
(b) (i) air in suburbs is better quality than in the inner city
(ii) air pollution can be unbearable in the summer in the inner city

(c) (i) Positive: (*either one*) lots of sports facilities / sports clubs, stadiums and swimming pools / cafés and shops good / good value / geared towards young people

(ii) Negative: Saturday nights often trouble in the town centre

(d) going to a concert

(e) a lot of cars and lorries at rush hour so queues

57. Weather

21 (a) B   (b) D   (c) A   (d) F
(e) C

22 (a) C   (b) B   (c) B

58. Celebrations at home

23 (a)
Gift – 3
What will happen after the ceremony – 1
Accommodation – 2

(b) wedding party / celebration

(c) (i) and (ii) (*any two of*) food / drink / music / fireworks

(d) extremely generous

24 (a) D   (b) B

59. Directions

25 (a) library
(b) crossroads
(c) right
(d) hospital

26 (a) D   (b) B   (c) F   (d) G

60. At the train station

27 (a) A   (b) B   (c) G   (d) F

28 (a) E   (b) D   (c) A

61. Travelling

29 (a) D   (b) A   (c) F   (d) I

30 (a) his parents think it is environmentally unfriendly / not good for the environment

(b) it's too far to cycle

(c) B

(d) C

62. Transport

31 (a) P + N   (b) P   (c) P + N
(d) N   (e) P

32 (a) people talking on their mobile phones

(b) quick and warm

(c) *advantage*: really comfortable; *disadvantage*: if the plane doesn't leave on time / punctually / waiting in airport for delayed plane / departure

(d) doesn't have to sit in traffic jams

63. The environment

33 (a) the building of a new motorway on the edge of town

(b) better public transport

(c) (i) air pollution will become as bad as in Bangkok or Mexico City

(ii) many people will suffer noise pollution

(d) (i) animals and plants will be protected

(ii) air quality in inner city and around outskirts will be preserved

34 **Sabine**
Main concern environmental pollution
Why emissions from factories and cars are highly damaging
Solution they need to be reduced immediately
Michael
Main concern over-population
Why as population grows there is not enough food / drink for them all
Solution education so people don't have as many children

64. Environmental issues

35 (a) 4   (b) 1   (c) 6   (d) 2

36 (a) F   (b) D   (c) A

65. What I do to be 'green'

37 (a) 11   (b) 25   (c) 8   (d) 18

38 (a) (i) wanted to recycle an old computer

(ii) needed to drive to the recycling tip as it was outside the town

(b) (i) no room left in wardrobe for clothes

(ii) (*either one*) wanted to give her old clothes to needy children / cousins already get the latest fashions

66. News headlines

39 (a) B   (b) B   (c) C
(d) A   (e) B

40 (a) poverty in Germany

(b) an environmental disaster

(c) effects of alcohol / drink on teenagers and adults

Work and education

67. School subjects

1 (a) M   (b) A   (c) J   (d) L

2 Llayda – E 3
Celina – B 1
Romeo – A 2
Eva – C 2

68. Opinions about school

3 (a) A **(b)** B **(c)** A **(d)** B
4 (a) N **(b)** P + N **(c)** P **(d)** P
5 B, D, F, H

69. School routine

6 (a) E **(b)** A **(c)** F **(d)** G

70. German schools

7 A, G, D, E
8 (a) (i) quiet / peaceful
  (ii) liked that she could wear what she wanted
(b) Positive: (*either one*) choice of after school activities / you can do sport, music, art club each evening
Negative: (*any one of*) tiring school day / get back home at 6 after clubs / school day finishes at 3.20

71. Primary school

9 Ben – B
  Tom – C
  Lena – D
  Susi – I
  Eric – F
  Jens – H
10 (a) A **(b)** E **(c)** C

72. Rules at school

11 (a) B **(b)** C **(c)** B **(d)** A
12 (a) D **(b)** B **(c)** F **(d)** G

73. School problems

13 (a) P **(b)** M **(c)** D **(d)** R
14 (a) P **(b)** N **(c)** P + N **(d)** P

74. Future education plans

15 (a) (wrote the) final exam (for her GCSEs)
(b) she needs excellent grades to get into the best sixth form in the area
(c) so she is ready to work hard in September
(d) she changed her mind from wanting to be a nurse to wanting to work with animals
(e) study veterinary medicine
(f) (*either one*) gain new experience / become independent

75. Future careers

16 (a) ? **(b)** T **(c)** ? **(d)** T
  (e) ? **(f)** F **(g)** T **(h)** ? **(i)** F

76. Jobs

17 Bettina – D
  Hugo – G
  Ellie – F
  Paul – A

18 (a) fun but tiring
(b) liked animals when he was a child
(d) to be a teacher
(d) it's the family business

77. Job adverts

19 (a) (*either one*) apply for a job with them/the restaurant today / become a waiter
(b) (i) and **(ii)** (*any two of*) modern restaurant / great colleagues / great working conditions / excellent opportunities
(c) (i) and **(ii)** (*any two of*) recently opened / Italian / near cathedral
(d) (*either one*) come in to collect application form today / send form plus CV by Monday 12 March
20 (a) D **(b)** G **(c)** H
(d) (*any order*) C, E

78. CV

21 (*any order*) C, E, H, I
22 (a) 14 January 2001
(b) grammar school
(c) hospital
(d) (*either one*) dancing / drama (theatre)

79. Job application

23 B, F, A, H
24 (a) C
(b) half past eleven / 11.30 am
(c) smart
(d) at home

80. Job interview

25 (a)
(i) do a German course
(ii) this year
(b) (i) and **(ii)** (*any two of*) gets on with people / helpful / friendly
26 (a) C **(b)** B **(c)** B **(d)** C
(e) B

81. Opinions about jobs

27 (a) S **(b)** E **(c)** S + E **(d)** E
28 (a) standing outside the changing room
(b) shout (loudly) at staff (in front of customers)
(c) (i) 30 days holiday per year
  (ii) 10% discount on all departments in the store

82. Part-time work

29 (a) delivering newspapers
(b) getting up so early
(c) (*either one*) he is tired in the evenings / long hours

(d) (*either one*) working on the till / talking to customers

(e) in his uncle's (Turkish) restaurant

(f) he can work as a waiter (rather than just wash up)

(g) being outside

(h) she wants to be a gardener later

83. Work experience

30 (a) B   **(b)** 8   **(c)** (very) nice   **(d)** A

31 (a) C   **(b)** A   **(c)** B   **(d)** A

84. My work experience

32 (a) F   **(b)** T   **(c)** ?   **(d)** T   **(e)** F
     (f) ?   **(g)** T   **(h)** F

33 (a) G   **(b)** A   **(c)** B   **(d)** C

Grammar

85. Gender and plurals

A
1. der Mülleimer
2. das Kino
3. die Krankenschwester
4. der Rucksack
5. das Handy
6. das Restaurant
7. die Autobahn
8. der Sportlehrer
9. die Umwelt

B
1. Das Haus ist modern.
2. Der Schüler heißt Max.
3. Die Schülerin heißt Demet.
4. Der Computer ist kaputt.
5. Der Zug fährt langsam.
6. Die Sparkasse ist geschlossen.
7. Die Zeitung kostet 1 Euro.
8. Das Buch ist langweilig.

C
1. Wir haben die Pizza gegessen.
2. Wir können das Krankenhaus sehen.
3. Ich mache die Hausaufgaben.
4. Vati kauft den Pullover.
5. Liest du das Buch?
6. Ich mähe den Rasen.

D Haus S, Buch S, Männer P, Autos P, Häuser P, Supermarkt S, Tisch S, Mann S, Supermärkte P, Tische P, Handys P, Zimmer E, Bilder P, Computer E

86. Cases 1

A
1. um die Ecke
2. durch die Stadt
3. ohne ein Auto
4. für die Schule
5. für einen Freund
6. gegen die Wand
7. durch einen Wald

B
1. mit dem Bus
2. seit dem Sommer
3. zu der Bank / zur Bank
4. nach der Party
5. bei einem Freund
6. von einem Onkel
7. gegenüber der Tankstelle
8. außer der Lehrerin

C
1. wegen des Wetters
2. während der Stunde
3. trotz des Regens

87. Cases 2

A
1. Wir fahren in die Stadt.
2. Meine Schwester ist in der Schule.
3. Das Essen steht auf dem Tisch.
4. Ich steige auf die Mauer.
5. Wir hängen das Bild an die Wand.
6. Jetzt ist das Bild an der Wand.
7. Die Katze läuft hinter einen Schrank.
8. Wo ist die Katze jetzt? Hinter dem Schrank.
9. Die Bäckerei steht zwischen einem Supermarkt und einer Post.
10. Das Flugzeug fliegt über die Stadt.
OR Das Flugzeug fliegt über der Stadt.
11. Ich stelle die Flaschen in den Schrank.
12. Der Bus steht an der Haltestelle.

B
1. Die Kinder streiten sich über das Fernsehprogramm.
2. Wir freuen uns auf das Festival.
3. Ich ärgere mich oft über die Arbeit.
4. Martin hat sich an die Sonne gewöhnt.
5. Wie lange warten Sie auf die Straßenbahn?

1. The children are arguing about the TV programme.
2. We are looking forward to the festival.
3. I often get cross about work.
4. Martin has got used to the sun.
5. How long have you been waiting for the tram?

C
1. auf dem Land – *in the country*
2. vor allem – *above all*
3. auf die Nerven – *on my nerves*
4. auf der rechten Seite – *on the right*
5. im Internet – *on the internet*

88. Cases 3

A
1. *this man* – dieser Mann
2. *with this man* – mit diesem Mann
3. *this woman* – diese Frau
4. *for this woman* – für diese Frau
5. *that horse* – jenes Pferd
6. *on that horse* – auf jenem Pferd

B
1. Unsere Schwester heißt Monika.
2. Ich habe keinen Bruder.
3. Meine Schule ist nicht sehr groß.
4. Hast du deinen Laptop vergessen?

5   Wie ist Ihr Name, bitte? *(No ending necessary)*
6   Meine Lehrerin hat ihre Schulbücher nicht mit.
7   Wo steht Ihr Auto? *(No ending necessary)*
8   Wir arbeiten in unserem Büro.
9   Wo ist eure Wohnung? *(Note spelling change)*
10 Meine Lieblingsfächer sind Mathe und Informatik.
11 Wie heißt deine Freundin?
12 Leider haben wir keine Zeit.
13 Ihre E-Mail war nicht sehr höflich.
14 Olaf geht mit seinem Freund spazieren.
15 Madonna singt ihre besten Hits.
16 Wo habt ihr euer Auto stehen lassen? *(No ending necessary)*
17 Ich habe keine Ahnung.
18 Ich habe keine Lust.
19 Das war mein Fehler.
20 Meiner Meinung nach …

89. Adjective endings

A   1   Die intelligente Schülerin bekommt gute Noten.
2   Wir fahren mit dem nächsten Bus in die Stadt.
3   Hast du den gelben Vogel gesehen?
4   Der altmodische Lehrer ist streng.
5   Ich kaufe dieses schwarze Kleid.
6   Die neugebauten Reihenhäuser sind schön.
7   Heute gehen wir in den modernen Freizeitpark.
8   Wir müssen dieses schmutzige Fahrrad sauber machen.
9   Morgen gehen wir ins neue Einkaufszentrum.
10 Der verspätete Zug kommt um ein Uhr an.

B   1   München ist eine umweltfreundliche Stadt.
2   Ich suche ein preiswertes T-Shirt.
3   Marta hat ihre modische Handtasche verloren.
4   Wir haben unsere schwierigen Hausaufgaben nicht gemacht.
5   Ich habe ein bequemes Bett gekauft.
6   Das ist ein großes Problem.
7   Das war vielleicht eine langweilige Stunde!
8   Diese idiotischen Leute haben das Spiel verdorben.
9   Mein Vater hat einen schweren Unfall gehabt.
10 Klaus liebt seine neue Freundin.
11 Wir haben kein frisches Obst.
12 Maria hat einen grünen Mantel gekauft.

90. Comparisons

A   1   Mathe ist langweilig, Physik ist langweiliger, aber das langweiligste Fach ist Kunst.
2   Oliver läuft schnell, Ali läuft schneller, aber Tim läuft am schnellsten.
3   Berlin ist schön, Paris ist schöner, aber Venedig ist die schönste Stadt.
4   Madonna ist cool, Lady Gaga ist cooler, aber Beyoncé ist die coolste Sängerin.
5   Metallica ist lauter als Guns N' Roses.
6   Bremen ist kleiner als Hamburg.
7   Deine Noten sind schlecht, aber meine sind noch schlechter.
8   Ich finde Englisch einfacher als Französisch, aber Deutsch finde ich am einfachsten.
9   Skifahren ist schwieriger als Radfahren.
10 Mein Auto ist billiger als dein Auto, aber das Auto meines Vaters ist am billigsten.

B   1   Ich bin jünger als du.
2   Die Alpen sind höher als der Snowdon.
3   München ist größer als Bonn.
4   Meine Haare sind lang, Timos Haare sind länger, aber deine Haare sind am längsten.
5   Fußball ist gut, Handball ist besser, aber Tennis ist das beste Spiel.

1   I am younger than you.
2   The Alps are higher than Snowdon.
3   Munich is bigger than Bonn.
4   My hair is long, Timo's hair is longer but your hair is the longest.
5   Football is good, handball is better but tennis is the best game.

C   1   Ich spiele gern Korbball.
2   Ich esse lieber Gemüse als Fleisch.
3   Am liebsten gehe ich schwimmen.

91. Personal pronouns

A   1   Ich liebe dich.
2   Liebst du mich?
3   Kommst du mit mir?
4   Mein Bruder ist nett. Ich mag ihn gern.
5   Ich habe keine Kreditkarte. Ich habe sie verloren.
6   Ein Geschenk für uns? Danke!
7   Wir haben euch gestern gesehen.
8   Haben Sie gut geschlafen?
9   Die Party ist bei mir.
10 Rolf hat Hunger. Ich bin mit ihm essen gegangen.
11 Vergiss mich nicht!
12 Wie heißt du?
13 Wie heißen Sie?
14 Meine Schwester ist krank. Gestern sind wir zu ihr gegangen.
15 Was ist los mit dir?

B
1 Schwimmen fällt mir schwer.
2 Mmmm, Eis! Schmeckt es dir?
3 Aua! Das tut mir weh!
4 Leider geht es uns nicht gut.
5 Wer gewinnt im Fußball? Das ist mir egal.
6 Es tut uns leid.

92. Word order

A
1 Um sechs Uhr beginnt die Fernsehsendung.
2 Jeden Tag fahre ich mit dem Bus zur Arbeit.
3 Leider sind meine Eltern krank.
4 Hier darf man nicht rauchen.

B
1 Gestern haben wir Eis gegessen.
2 Manchmal ist Timo ins Kino gegangen.
3 Letztes Jahr ist Ali nach Frankreich gefahren.
4 Heute Morgen hast du Pommes gekauft.

C
1 Ich fahre jeden Tag mit dem Rad zur Schule.
2 Gehst du am Wochenende mit mir ins Schwimmbad?
3 Wir sehen oft im Wohnzimmer fern.
4 Mehmet spielt abends im Jugendklub Tischtennis.
5 Mein Vater arbeitet seit 20 Jahren fleißig im Büro.
6 Willst du heute Abend mit mir im Restaurant Pizza essen?

93. Conjunctions

A
1 Claudia will Sportlehrerin werden, weil sie sportlich ist.
2 Ich kann dich nicht anrufen, weil ich mein Handy verloren habe.
3 Wir fahren nach Spanien, weil das Wetter dort so schön ist.
4 Du darfst nicht im Garten spielen, weil es regnet.
5 Peter hat seine Hausaufgaben nicht gemacht, weil er faul ist.
6 Ich mag Computerspiele, weil sie so spannend sind.

B
1 Du kannst abwaschen, während ich koche.
2 Wir kaufen oft ein, wenn wir in der Stadt sind.
3 Ich kann nicht zur Party kommen, da ich arbeiten werde.
4 Lasst uns früh aufstehen, damit wir wandern können.
5 Meine Eltern waren böse, obwohl ich nicht spät nach Hause gekommen bin.
6 Ich habe es nicht gewusst, dass du krank bist.
7 Papa hat geraucht, als er jung war.
8 Ich weiß nicht, wie man einen Computer repariert.

9 Wir können schwimmen gehen, wenn das Wetter gut ist.
10 Wir müssen warten, bis es nicht mehr regnet.

94. More on word order

A
1 Wir fahren in die Stadt, um Lebensmittel zu kaufen.
2 Viele Leute spielen Tennis, um fit zu werden.
3 Boris spart Geld, um ein Motorrad zu kaufen.
4 Meine Schwester geht zur Abendschule, um Französisch zu lernen.
5 Ich bin gestern zum Imbiss gegangen, um Pommes zu essen.

B
1 Das Orchester beginnt zu spielen.
2 Wir hoffen, Spanisch zu lernen.
3 Oliver versucht, Gitarre zu spielen.

C
1 das Mädchen, das Tennis spielt
2 der Junge, der gut singt
3 der Mann, der Deutsch spricht
4 das Haus, das alt ist
5 das Fach, das schwer ist
6 das Auto, das kaputt ist
7 die Tasse, die voll ist

95. The present tense

A
1 wir gehen 2 er findet
3 sie singt 4 ich spiele
5 ihr macht 6 du sagst
7 es kommt 8 sie schwimmen
9 ich höre 10 wir trinken

B
1 Was liest du?
2 Schläfst du?
3 Annabelle isst nicht gern Fleisch.
4 Kerstin spricht gut Englisch.
5 Nimmst du Zucker?
6 Ben fährt bald nach Berlin.
7 Hilfst du mir bitte?
8 Mein Onkel gibt mir 20 Euro.

1 What are you reading?
2 Are you asleep?
3 Annabelle doesn't like eating meat.
4 Kerstin speaks English well.
5 Do you take sugar?
6 Ben is going to Berlin soon.
7 Will you help me please?
8 My uncle is giving me 20 euros.

C er spricht, du siehst, sie fährt, er liest

96. More on verbs

A
1 Wir waschen ab.
2 Er wacht um 7 Uhr auf.
3 Wir laden oft Filme herunter.
4 Wie oft siehst du fern?
5 Wo steigt man aus?

6   Ich wasche nie ab.
B   1   Wir haben abgewaschen.
     2   Er ist um 7 Uhr aufgewacht.
     3   Wir haben oft Filme heruntergeladen.
     4   Wie oft hast du ferngesehen?
     5   Wo ist man ausgestiegen?
     6   Ich habe nie abgewaschen.
C   1   Ich interessiere mich für Geschichte.
     2   Sara freut sich auf die Ferien.
     3   Erinnerst du dich an mich?
     4   Wir langweilen uns in der Schule.
     5   Ich habe mich noch nicht entschieden.
     6   Dieter hat sich heute noch nicht rasiert.
     7   Habt ihr euch gut amüsiert?
     8   Unser Haus befindet sich in der Nähe
          vom Bahnhof.

     1   I am interested in history.
     2   Sara is looking forward to the holidays.
     3   Do you remember me?
     4   We get bored at school.
     5   I haven't decided yet.
     6   Dieter hasn't shaved yet today.
     7   Have you enjoyed yourselves?
     8   Our house is situated near the train station.

97. Commands

A   1   Parken Sie hier nicht!
     2   Sprechen Sie nicht so laut!
     3   Steigen Sie hier aus!
     4   Fahren Sie nicht so schnell!
     5   Kommen Sie herein!
     6   Gehen Sie geradeaus!
     7   Kommen Sie bald wieder!
     8   Geben Sie mir 10 Euro!

B   1   Steh auf!
     2   Schreib bald!
     3   Komm her!
     4   Nimm zwei!
     5   Bring mir den Ball!
     6   Hör auf!
     7   Benimm dich!
     8   Setz dich!

98. Present tense modals

A   1   Ich kann nicht schnell laufen.
     2   Wir müssen bald Kaffee kaufen.
     3   Kinder sollten keinen Alkohol trinken.
     4   Claudia mag nicht schwimmen.
     5   Schüler dürfen hier nicht sitzen.
     6   Wir wollen Pommes essen.
     7   Hier darf man parken.
     8   Meine Eltern wollen eine neue Wohnung
          kaufen.
     9   Du kannst gut Fußball spielen.
     10   Sie sollten höflich sein.
B   1   Im Kino darf man nicht rauchen.
     2   Wir können zur Bowlingbahn gehen.

3   Meine Freunde wollen zu Hause bleiben.
4   Ihr müsst weniger essen.
5   Wir wollen nach München fahren.
6   Ergül kann gut Gitarre spielen.
7   Kannst du mir bei meinen Hausaufgaben
     helfen?
8   Man darf den Rasen nicht betreten.
9   Wir müssen mit der Straßenbahn fahren.
10   Ich will meinen Salat nicht essen.

99. Imperfect modals

A   1   ich wollte   2   wir mussten
     3   sie konnten   4   sie durfte
     5   man sollte   6   er mochte
     7   wir wollten   8   Jutta konnte
B   1   Du konntest mitspielen.
     2   Wir mussten nach Hause gehen.
     3   Ella mochte nicht Musik hören.
     4   Wir wollten im Internet surfen.
     5   Ich konnte gut Tischtennis spielen.
     6   Ihr durftet spät ins Bett gehen.
C   1   Möchten Sie Tennis spielen?
     2   Wir könnten einkaufen gehen.
     3   Ich möchte ein Eis essen.
     4   Könntest du mir helfen?

100. The perfect tense 1

A   1   Wir haben Minigolf gespielt.
     2   Habt ihr neue Schuhe gekauft?
     3   Hast du deine Oma besucht?
     4   Was hat er gesagt?
     5   Ich habe Spanisch gelernt.
     6   Hast du Harry Potter gelesen?
     7   Dennis hat mir ein Geschenk gegeben.
     8   Wir haben einen tollen Film gesehen.
B   1   Wohin bist du gefahren?
     2   Wir sind nach Mallorca gefahren.
     3   Ich bin zu Hause geblieben.
     4   Usain Bolt ist schnell gelaufen.
     5   Meine Mutter ist nach Amerika geflogen.
     6   Der Zug ist abgefahren.
C   1   Abdul hat 12 Stunden geschlafen.
     2   Wir haben unsere Hausaufgaben gemacht.
     3   Wohin bist du gefahren?
     4   Ich bin spät nach Hause gekommen.
     5   Habt ihr Britta gesehen?

101. The perfect tense 2

A   1   geschwommen   2   gewesen
     3   geschlossen   4   gegessen
     5   gestanden   6   gesessen
     7   geschrieben   8   gestorben
     9   gesprochen   10   getroffen
     11   geworden   12   getrunken
     13   genommen   14   gesungen
     15   gehabt
B   1   Wir haben eine E-Mail geschrieben.

129

2 Wir haben uns um 6 Uhr getroffen.
3 Mein Onkel ist gestorben.
4 Hast du mein Handy genommen?
5 Ich habe eine Bratwurst gegessen.
6 Er hat ein Glas Cola getrunken.
7 Wir sind im Meer geschwommen.
8 Marita hat Italienisch gesprochen.

C 1 vergessen 2 aufgestanden
3 empfohlen 4 verloren
5 besucht 6 heruntergeladen
7 abgefahren 8 ausgestiegen

102. The imperfect tense

A 1 Ich spielte am Computer.
2 Was sagtest du?
3 Nina kaufte Kaugummi.
4 Die Schüler lernten Englisch.
5 Es schneite im Winter.
6 Peter lachte laut.

B 1 Es war gestern kalt.
2 Wir hatten auf der Party viel Spaß.
3 Paul war im Krankenhaus.
4 Ihre Eltern hatten drei Kinder.
5 Ich war gestern im Imbiss.
6 Hattest du Angst?

C 1 Es gab viel zu essen. I
2 Wir sitzen im Kino. P
3 Es tut mir leid! P
4 Ich fahre nach Berlin. P
5 Er kommt früh an. P
6 Er saß im Wohnzimmer. I
7 Sie kamen um 6 Uhr an. I
8 Wie findest du das? P
9 Aua! Das tat weh! I
10 Ich fand es gut. I
11 Es gibt nicht viel zu tun. P
12 Klaus fuhr zu schnell. I

103. The future tense

A 1 Susi geht nächstes Jahr auf die Uni.
2 Wir fahren im Sommer nach Ibiza.
3 Er kommt übermorgen zu uns.
4 Ich bleibe heute Abend zu Hause.
5 Bringst du am Wochenende deine
Schwester mit?

B 1 Ich werde um 6 Uhr aufstehen.
2 Wirst du am Wochenende Musik hören?
3 Werdet ihr Pizza essen?
4 Wir werden die Prüfung bestehen.
5 Nächstes Jahr werden wir nach Afrika
fahren.
6 Daniel wird einen Film herunterladen.
7 Ich werde ein Problem mit meinem
Laptop haben.
8 Bayern München wird das Spiel gewinnen.
9 Meine Freunde werden um 9 Uhr
ankommen.
10 Meine Schwester wird im August
heiraten.

C *Answers variable!*

104. The conditional

A 1 Wenn wir Zeit hätten, würden wir
einkaufen gehen.
2 Wenn meine Eltern Geld hätten, würden
sie ein Auto kaufen.
3 Wenn ich Kinder hätte, würde ich sie
lieben.
4 Wenn Tanja nicht krank wäre, würde sie
Skateboard fahren.
5 Wenn du fleißiger wärst, würdest du
deine Prüfung bestehen.
6 Wenn das Wetter besser wäre, würden
wir Sport treiben.

B 1 Wenn ich Krankenschwester wäre, würde
ich mich freuen.
2 Wenn er Klempner wäre, würde er viel
verdienen.
3 Wenn wir in einer Fabrik arbeiten
würden, wären wir müde.
4 Wenn wir Glasflaschen hätten, würden
wir sie recyceln.
5 Wenn ich Hunger hätte, würde ich eine
Bratwurst essen.
6 Wenn Manya und Timo Talent hätten,
würden sie in einer Band spielen.

C *Answers variable!*

D *Answers variable!*

105. The pluperfect tense

A 1 Wir hatten Kaffee und Kuchen bestellt.
2 Hattest du Spaß gehabt?
3 Ich hatte eine neue Stelle bekommen.
4 Wir hatten unsere Freunde eingeladen.
5 Nachdem ich nach Hause gekommen
war, habe ich gegessen.
6 Ergül war zur Bäckerei gegangen.
7 Sie waren zu Hause geblieben.
8 Ich war mit dem Auto nach Frankfurt
gefahren.

B 1 Es war überhaupt nicht passiert.
2 Ich hatte dir eine E-Mail geschickt.
3 Hattest du dich nicht rasiert?
4 Ich war sehr früh eingeschlafen.
5 Opa war noch nie nach London gefahren.
6 Warst du zur Haltestelle gegangen?
7 Wir hatten unseren Müll zur Mülldeponie
gebracht.
8 Er hatte zwei Computerspiele
heruntergeladen.
9 Die Fabrik war geschlossen worden.
10 Fatima hatte Abitur gemacht.

106. Questions

A
1 Spielt Kevin oft am Computer?
2 Hast du dein Handy verloren?
3 Wollen wir Volleyball spielen?
4 Studiert Hakan Informatik?
5 Geht ihr morgen zum Sportzentrum?

B
1 Bist du zum Supermarkt gefahren?
2 Wird Ayse Chemie studieren?
3 Ist dein Auto kaputt?
4 Isst du gern Bratwurst mit Pommes?
5 Wird es morgen regnen?

C
who? – wer?   what? – was?
how? – wie?   when? – wann?
why? – warum?   where? – wo?

how many? – wie viele?
what kind of? – was für?
whose? – wessen?
who with? – mit wem?

D *Answers variable!*

107. Time markers

A
1 gestern – *past*
2 früher – *past*
3 bald – *future*
4 letzte Woche – *past*
5 heute – *present*
6 normalerweise – *present*
7 vor 2 Wochen – *past*
8 morgen – *future*
9 nächste Woche – *future*
10 jetzt – *present*

B
manchmal – *sometimes*
neulich – *recently*
sofort – *immediately*
täglich – *every day*
rechtzeitig – *on time*
in Zukunft – *in the future*

C
1 Nächste Woche werde ich mein Betriebspraktikum machen.
2 Heute Abend sieht Ulli fern.
3 In Zukunft wird man Strom sparen.
4 Bald wirst du einen Unfall haben.
5 Manchmal treffen wir uns mit unseren Freunden.
6 Neulich war ich bei meinem Onkel.
7 Vorgestern hat Mehmet sein Betriebspraktikum begonnen.
8 Jeden Tag gehe ich zur Bäckerei.

108. Numbers

A
1 421
2 1644
3 68
4 301
5 97
6 105
7 17
8 653

B
1 Es ist zwanzig nach neun. (20, 9)
2 Ausverkauf! Fünfzehn Prozent Rabatt! (15)
3 Es ist dreizehn Grad. (13)
4 Ich habe sechshundertfünfzig Euro gewonnen. (650)
5 Der Zug kommt um zwölf Minuten vor sieben an. (12, 7)
6 Es gibt dreißig Schüler in meiner Klasse. (30)

C
1 12.3.   **2** 13.7.   **3** 28.12.
4 1.4.   **5** 3.1.   **6** 17.6.

D
1 Mein Geburtstag ist am ersten November.
2 Saschas Geburtstag ist am siebten September.
3 Das Konzert findet am zwölften Mai statt.
4 Die Ferien beginnen am zweiten Juli.

Practice Exam Paper

109. Reading

1 **(a)** D   **(b)** B   **(c)** G   **(d)** C

2 **(a)** station
(b) pedestrian area
(c) tourist information office
(d) library

3 **(a)** 5
(b) very loud
(c) (i) and **(ii)** (*any two of*) very funny / brown hair / green eyes
(d) curly

4 **(a)** D   **(b)** F   **(c)** G   **(d)** B

5 (*any order*) B, C, F, I

6 **(a)** E   **(b)** B   **(c)** M   **(d)** H

7 **(a)** T   **(b)** ?   **(c)** ?   **(d)** ?   **(e)** F
(f) F   **(g)** ?   **(h)** T

8 **(a)** A   **(b)** C   **(c)** B   **(d)** B

9 **(a) (i)** Positive: (*either*) friendly spectators / her dad buys her sausage and chips
    (ii) Negative: no commentator to explain complicated rules
(b) (*either*) it is it without doubt her sport number one / it is a lot of fun
(c) increased from two to four times training each week
(d) she doesn't want to lose her place at the club
(e) to relax

114. Listening

1 **(a)** C   **(b)** C   **(c)** A   **(d)** B

2 **(a)** Geography
(b) Thursday

    (c) 2 o'clock / 14:00

    (d) badminton

3 (*any order*) B, E, F, G

4 **(a)** C, A   **(b)** I   **(c)** D

5 **(a)** (fresh) coffee
    (b) (*one of*) fruit / sausage / cheese / bread
    (c) 13 (euros)
    (d) 7.30 am

6 **(a)** E   **(b)** A   **(c)** F   **(d)** B

7 **(a)** B   **(b)** B   **(c)** C   **(d)** A

8 **(a)** P + N   **(b)** N   **(c)** P   **(d)** P + N

9 **(a)** B   **(b)** C   **(c)** A   **(d)** C

10 **(a)** skiing

    (b) **(i)** and **(ii)** (*any two of*) fast cable car /
    ski lift / fantastic views / winter sports /
    unforgettable skiing holidays

    (c) people who want to learn to (*any one of*)
    surf / sail / climb

11 **(a)** C   **(b)** E   **(c)** D

Your own notes

Published by Pearson Education Limited, Edinburgh Gate, Harlow, Essex, CM20 2JE.

www.pearsonschoolsandfecolleges.co.uk

Text © Pearson Education Limited 2013
Audio recorded at Tom Dick and Debbie Productions, © Pearson Education Limited
MFL Series Editor Julie Green
Edited by Jenny Draine and Sue Chapple
Typeset by Kamae Design, Oxford
Original illustrations © Pearson Education Limited 2013
Illustrations by John Hallett
Cover illustration by Miriam Sturdee

The rights of Harriette Lanzer and Oliver Gray to be identified as authors of this work have been asserted by them in accordance with the Copyright, Designs and Patents Act 1988.

The authors and publishers are grateful to Olwyn Bowpitt for the use of some original material.
First published 2013

16 15 14
10 9 8 7 6 5 4 3

British Library Cataloguing in Publication Data
A catalogue record for this book is available from the British Library

ISBN 978 1 447 94114 9

Printed in Slovakia by Neografia

In the writing of this book, no AQA examiners authored sections relevant to examination papers for which they have responsibility.